The
History *of*
Theological
Education

The
History *of*
Theological
Education

Justo L. González

🔊|Abingdon Press

Nashville

This book is printed on acid-free paper.

Library of Congress Cataloging-in-Publication Data

González, Justo L.
    The history of theological education / Justo L. González.
    Includes bibliographical references and index.
    ISBN 978-1-4267-8191-9 (binding: soft back, pbk./trade : alk. paper)
    1. Theology—Study and teaching—History. 2. Theology—Study and teaching—United States.
I. Title.
    BV4023.G66 2015
    230.071—dc23

2014039938

All scripture quotations unless otherwise noted are taken from the New Revised Standard Version of the Bible, copyright 1989, Division of Christian Education of the National Council of the Churches of Christ in the United States of America. Used by permission. All rights reserved.

Primary source quotations marked AT are the author's own translations of the works.

15 16 17 18 19 20 21 22 23 24—10 9 8 7 6 5 4 3 2 1
MANUFACTURED IN THE UNITED STATES OF AMERICA

Contents

vii   Preface

ix   Introduction

1   1. The Early Church

9   2. The Catechumenate

15   3. From Constantine to the Germanic Invasions

23   4. The Romanization of the Germanic Peoples

29   5. Early Medieval Schools

37   6. The Beginnings of Scholasticism

43   7. The Universities and Scholasticism

55   8. The Last Centuries of the Middle Ages

63   9. In Quest of Alternatives

69   10. The Protestant Reformation

79   11. The Catholic Reformation

87   12. Protestant Scholasticism and Rationalism

95   13. The Pietist Reaction

105   14. Modern Theological Education

117   15. A Brief Overview

131   16. Bringing It Home

141   Notes

149   Index

Preface

A few years ago, I received an invitation from the Seminario Nacional Teológico Presbiteriano in Mexico City to conduct a workshop for its faculty and for colleagues in other institutions in Mexico. The subject they wished me to address was the history of theological education. Later, when I was invited by Columbia Theological Seminary, in Decatur, Georgia, to deliver their annual Smyth lectures, I took the opportunity to continue reflection on that subject and also to relate it more closely with the challenges that theological education faces in the United States.

This book is the result of my research and reflection for those occasions. Therefore I dedicate it to my colleague and friends, some in Mexico and some in Decatur, who either directly or indirectly have forced me to look anew at the history of theological education in the Christian church. Foremost among them is my wife, Dr. Catherine G. González, who is herself a professor emerita of church history at Columbia Theological Seminary and who had the patience to read my manuscript more than once and the grace and wisdom to suggest many valuable corrections.

To all of you, thank you!

Decatur
First Sunday in Advent, 2013

Introduction

This book is built on four basic premises. The first is that some form of theological education is part of the very essence of the church. The first great commandment calls on the church as a whole, and on every believer in particular, to love God with all our minds. This means that theological inquiry is not to be regarded as an interesting pastime for curious people but rather as an act of devotion and obedience to God. At the same time, however, the second great commandment implies that such inquiry is not to be only for our individual benefit but also for the benefit of others. The love of God is not really such without the love of neighbor. Therefore, good theology always has a communal dimension. It is developed within the context of the church as it seeks to experience and enjoy God and to proclaim God's love for the world.

Given this communal nature of theology, it follows that in a broad sense good theology is always expressed in theological education—in letting believers know what the church as a whole knows. Good theology seeks to communicate itself, to be part of the church, to bring other believers to know and experience what it knows and experiences.

This is the first premise of this book, that not only theology but also theological education is part of the essence of the church. Or, to put it bluntly, that a church without theology and theological education is falling far short of its calling.

The second premise is that theological education as we have understood it in the last few centuries is in crisis. While, as we shall see further on, this crisis is multidimensional, it may be verified by simply looking at enrollment in seminaries and schools of theology.

In this respect, the Roman Catholic crisis is profound. The lack of candidates for the priesthood is appalling. Very few traditionally Catholic countries—not even Ireland—produce enough priests to meet their own needs, much less to supply the needs of others. In Europe, the United States, and most of Latin America, seminaries and schools of theology that used to have hundreds of students now graduate less than a dozen a year. A few years ago, when I spoke at one of the most prestigious Catholic schools of theology in the United States, the graduating class included only eight candidates for the priesthood. Furthermore, the fewer priests there are, the more they must spend their time in ritual and sacramental functions, and the less personal contact they have with their flock. This in turn makes the priesthood even less attractive to young men considering a vocation of service, thus making the crisis even more acute.

Protestants are often tempted to think that the Roman Catholic crisis is due to clerical celibacy and the refusal to ordain women. Certainly, this is part of the equation. But it is not all of it. There is an old Spanish saying: *Cuando veas las bardas de tu vecino arder, pon las tuyas en remojo*—when you see your neighbor's fence burning, douse yours, because neighbors have a common fence. The fire on the Catholic side of the fence is already smoldering on the Protestant side. In "mainline" Protestant denominations in the United States, the problem is not so much lack of pastors as it is lack of pulpits as rural churches disappear or merge, as congregations decline in urban settings, and as the ordained ministry loses the social prestige it had a few decades ago. As a result, denominational seminaries are finding recruitment of candidates for ordination among their traditional constituencies ever more difficult. In many, the crisis is hidden by one or more of three factors or strategies. The first is the—still relatively small—recruitment of ethnic minorities. In some Presbyterian and Methodist schools, the influx of Korean students ameliorates the situation, while in a few seminaries of other denominations the presence of Hispanic students has the same effect. Second, a number of mainline seminaries have turned to recruiting students from denominations that do not require an MDiv degree for ordination and developing programs for them. Third, some institutions have developed DMin programs that temporarily bring up their numbers—although it is evident that, as the pool of people with an MDiv diminishes, recruitment for the DMin will become ever more difficult and competitive.

If to such issues in recruitment one adds financial difficulties, questions regarding relevance, and the fact that the churches that have traditionally required a seminary degree are by and large the same denominations whose membership is rapidly declining, it is clear that theological education as commonly conceived—essentially as the work of educational institutions dedicated to training for the ordained ministry and accredited by organizations such as the Association of Theological Schools (ATS)—is in crisis.

The third premise serves to qualify the second, for it is that, while theological education in the sense of that traditional establishment is in crisis, theological education in a wider sense is not. The day after I spoke at that Catholic school of theology graduating eight candidates for the priesthood, I attended the graduation of a lay training program conducted in the same city and mostly by the same faculty. There was row upon row of graduates, and the crowd attending the event filled the cathedral to overflowing. Likewise, some years ago The United Methodist Publishing House produced a series of studies—DISCIPLE: BECOMING DISCIPLES THROUGH BIBLE STUDY (1), DISCIPLE: INTO THE WORD INTO THE WORLD (2), and so forth—that required participants to make a firm commitment to weeks of study and participation in group sessions. Its success has been spectacular, expanding far beyond the limits of The United Methodist Church. The recent release of Covenant Bible Study is another example of committed learning and the cultivation of faith's wisdom in a small group context. Like DISCIPLE, weekly gatherings add a conversational approach to scripture study that is disciplined by daily reading and informed by thoughtful video examples of scholars and pastors discussing the Bible around a shared table. Similar stories could be repeated almost ad infinitum. Everywhere there are programs of lay theological education, Bible study groups, online courses, and much more. And, in terms of numbers, most of them have little difficulty recruiting students. Indeed, in this context the crisis is not in recruitment but rather in quality control—in the proliferation of programs offered by those who, as Gregory the Great would say, "claim to be teachers of what they have never learned."

Finally, the fourth premise is that the study of the history of theological education—particularly of theological education in the wider sense—is one of the best tools we can use for guidance into the future. Such study will help us see that much that we take for granted as necessary may not be so—reminding us, for instance, that for fifteen centuries the church subsisted, taught its theology, and at times flourished, without a single seminary. It will warn us of some of the pitfalls into which others have stumbled. It will suggest new avenues and vistas for theological education—avenues patterned after past successes and avoiding past shortcomings and vistas widening the horizon and scope of theological education.

It is on the basis of these four premises—and of several others, probably many hidden even to myself—that this book is written.

1

The Early Church

As we look at the past of theological education, we must begin by acknowledging that the New Testament does not offer much useful data. There is no doubt that the years of Jesus's public ministry were a time during which his immediate followers were preparing for ministry. Later on, when Peter suggests that somebody be chosen to fill the vacancy left by Judas (Acts 1:15-26), he sets requirements for that post. (Interestingly, one of these requirements is that the candidate must have been with Jesus since the very beginning of his ministry to the very end, and this is a requirement that very few among the eleven fill.) So they cast lots in order to elect this new person—not a method many would recommend today! Later the congregation in Jerusalem chooses seven, but we are not told what training or formation the seven may have had. Furthermore, the seven are supposed to be administering the aid to the widows, but at least two of them—Stephen and Phillip—end up preaching. Still later Paul chooses Timothy, who has received some training from his mother and grandmother. The Pastoral Epistles mention some of the characteristics that bishops and deacons must have, but there is no word about how they are to be trained or taught.

Even after the period of the New Testament, we are told little about ministerial training, although there is much we may infer. First, there is no doubt that in order to lead worship one had to be able to read. Christian worship on Sunday mornings, which usually lasted several hours, had two parts, the Service of the Word and the Service of the Table. In order to lead in the latter, it was necessary to know at least something about the history of Israel and the work of God in the gospel, particularly since the person presiding had to lead in the great Eucharistic prayer, in which God was thanked for all the divine mercies, not only in the present but also from the very beginning of creation.

But in order to preside at the Service of the Word one had to know more. Certainly, it was necessary to know how to read, since most of the service consisted of scripture readings. We know that the literacy index in the Greco-Roman cities—which was where Christianity first made headway—was low, as might be expected. It is estimated that in the Latin-speaking provinces the index of literacy was between 5 and 10 percent.[1] But there are also indications that most people in the church were women, or men belonging to the lower echelons of society. Except in the very high levels of society, few Greco-Roman women knew how to read. Among slaves and artisans, who did not need to read and in any case would have little use for literacy, illiteracy was common. The main exceptions were the slaves who served as tutors for children in wealthy families—the pedagogues— and those merchants and artisans who had to use the rudiments of writing in order to keep their accounts and to sustain the communications necessary for their business. Therefore, there would be few among the members of the early church who knew how to read, and it was from among these few that bishops were elected, since one of the main functions of a bishop was to preside over worship. (Hermas, whose brother was bishop of Rome toward the middle of the second century, was a slave, although sufficiently learned to write the book that is known now as *The Shepherd*. Although he does not tell us what his duties were as a slave, it is quite likely that he was a pedagogue or at least an amanuensis for his masters. The status of his brother Pius is not known. Since Hermas was a slave, it is most likely that Pius was also a slave—or, if not, a freedman.)

Furthermore, the Service of the Word required not only the reading of scripture but also its interpretation. Those who had some secular studies, especially in the field of rhetoric, were particularly able to perform these functions, since a goodly part of rhetorical studies was devoted to the interpretation of ancient Greek and Roman poets and other authors. The principles of interpretation that would apply to those classical texts in the field of rhetoric were also useful for the interpretation of biblical passages during the Service of the Word. (This is why many of the allegorical interpretations of scripture that theologians of the time were prompt to offer, although very strange from our point of view, were perfectly acceptable for those who heard or read them. What these interpreters were doing with the Bible was similar to what secular orators of the time did with Homer or Hesiod.) In any case, the church had no school where it could teach people how to read, much less the principles to be applied in the interpretation of ancient texts. Therefore, one must conclude that most bishops had learned these matters in pagan schools.

Bishops were also the link joining the churches together. Since most contacts with other bishops had to take place through correspondence, this too required that bishops know how to read and write—or at least that they know the principles of writing sufficiently well to employ an amanuensis. Although most of this ancient correspondence has been lost, we have an example of this in the epistle the church of Rome wrote to that of Corinth through Bishop Clement of Rome, late in the first century. Slightly later, we have the seven letters of Ignatius of Antioch, five of them addressed to churches he had visited on his way to martyrdom, a sixth to the church of Rome, where he expected to die, and a seventh to young Bishop Polycarp of Smyrna. And even later, we have the correspondence that Polycarp sent to the Philippians. Among other bishops who took up writing, one may mention Papias of Hierapolis, who set for himself the task of collecting "sayings of the Lord," and Melito of Sardis, of whose many writings all that remains is a beautiful Easter sermon, possibly written in order to have it circulate among nearby churches. In 411, in an African synod gathered to condemn Donatism, there was only one bishop—Polainos of Zura—who was deemed "ignorant in letters,"[2] but it is not clear whether this means that he was actually illiterate or simply that he was not learned.

In brief, although there are many indications that a good number of the bishops of the second century were relatively learned people who at least knew how to read, how to interpret texts, and how to sustain a correspondence with their colleagues, there is no indication that the church had any schools for the training of such bishops or pastors.

Even when schools began to appear somewhat later, these schools were not intended for the training of pastors, for these were still elected without any other instruction than what they might have received in pagan schools as well as in the church itself, particularly in the Service of the Word. There are many examples that show these procedures, but in order to see how they functioned, it is well to review and compare the careers of two of the most distinguished theologians of the Western church, Ambrose and Augustine.

Although raised in a Christian home, and even though he himself was a faithful believer, Ambrose had not even been baptized when he was elected bishop of Milan. He had devoted his life to a career in civil service, and to that end he had been well educated, particularly in rhetoric. But now, much to his surprise, in the span of a week he was baptized and made a bishop. Immediately he called on Simplician, who was learned in matters of theology, to serve as his mentor and advisor on such matters. It is impossible to know how much of what Ambrose wrote he learned from Simplician and what he received from other sources. But the fact remains that, even when he hadn't attended any seminary or similar school, Ambrose devoted himself to studying theology, particularly by reading Greek writers such as Basil the Great, and eventually became one of the main exponents and defenders of trinitarian doctrine in the West. He also wrote a treatise *On the Duties of the Clergy* to which we shall return in another chapter.

As for Augustine, he too had no formal studies in theology before he was made first a presbyter and then a bishop. All the studies of his youth concentrated on classical rhetoric. As part of these studies, he read the writings of Cicero and of the Neoplatonic philosophers. But he did not pay attention to theological matters until after his conversion in 386, when he withdrew to Cassisiacum shortly before his baptism. Later Augustine founded in his native Tagaste a community dedicated to study and prayer, and he remained in that community until he was forced to accept ordination as a presbyter in 391. Between the time of his conversion and his ordination, Augustine wrote several theological treatises—among them *Against the Academics, On Order, On the Quantity of the Soul, On Free Will,* and *On the Customs of the Manicheans and of the Catholic Church.* It was perhaps the fame that he acquired thought these writings that led Bishop Valerius of Hippo to force him into the pastorate. But even when he was writing all these works, Augustine had no formal education in theology, and on a number of issues his early opinions still bore the stamp of Neoplatonism rather than Christianity. It was only through the passing of years, and faced by the need to study and expound Christian scriptures and teachings, that Augustine's theology was developed and refined.

Many other cases could be cited. Basil of Caesarea and Gregory of Nazianzus studied in the Academy of Athens—once again, only in the fields of rhetoric and philosophy. They eventually became very important theologians, but they were never formally students of theology.

As all of this was taking place, the distinction between presbyters and bishops was developing. The distinction between these two titles, originally synonymous, developed as the church grew in cities where a single bishop could no longer attend to the needs of the entire flock, and it became necessary to celebrate worship in various localities within the city. The presbyters then became aides to the bishop and his representatives in services where the bishop was absent. Through a natural process this distinction of rank developed—as did other functions and titles, such as that of reader—and led to the beginning of study programs under the supervision of the bishops. There is no indication that these programs of study were formal, but we do know that presbyters would read and practice what was recommended to them by the bishops, so that their work as presbyters took place under a sort of mentoring that might also prepare them for a possible election to the episcopate. In the third century, in the letters of Cyprian, we see that he used to examine the candidates to various orders, and these in turn had specific functions. At least some of the presbyters were teachers, and some among the readers were entrusted with the instruction of candidates for baptism. In a letter that Cyprian wrote to the presbyters and deacons under his supervision we also see, although only in passing, that Cyprian took charge of the training and

4

formation of the clergy under his supervision. Cyprian tells his presbyters and deacons:

> Know therefore that I have ordained Saturus as a reader, and Optatus as a confessor, both of whom, by common agreement, we had been preparing to be part of the clergy, since we have entrusted Saturus more than once with the reading on Easter, and later, as we examined carefully those who were to be readers and the teaching presbyters, we ordained Optatus as a reader to serve among those who instruct catechumens, and we have examined all the qualities that must abide in those that are training for the clergy.[3]

As for the bishops themselves, no one supervised their instruction, although we do know that by the middle of the second century it was customary that the one elected to be a bishop of a community would write a declaration of faith that would be sufficiently detailed to express his main beliefs and theology and that his prospective colleagues in nearby cities had the authority to determine whether the one who had been elected had the necessary knowledge and orthodoxy to fulfill faithfully the tasks that would be entrusted to him. In that case, several of those neighboring bishops would take part in the ordination of the new bishop, thus giving witness to their theological agreement with him. But even though there was this emphasis on the orthodoxy and the knowledge of prospective pastors, there were no schools devoted to their training.

Even so, there were already Christian schools. The most remarkable and the best known are the one that Justin Martyr founded in Rome and the famous catechetical school of Alexandria.

Justin's school was patterned after the philosophical schools of his time. He was convinced that Christianity was "the true philosophy," and his school was therefore devoted to expounding this philosophy. Not all who attended this particular school were Christians, for many came seeking after truth while others came out of mere curiosity. The only disciple of Justin of whom more is known is Tatian, who later, imitating his master but from a very different theological perspective, wrote against pagans in defense of Christianity and eventually founded a sect of Gnostic tendencies. As far as is known, neither Justin nor Tatian was ordained. We do know that as a result of the school and its fame, Justin was challenged to a debate by the pagan philosopher Crescentius, and it has been suggested that it was Crescentius who, having been bested by Justin, took revenge by accusing his rival before the authorities and thus caused his martyrdom.

A little more is known about the catechetical school of Alexandria, which lasted much longer than Justin's in Rome. Jerome claimed that it was founded by Saint Mark, but this may be discounted given the tendency in the times of Jerome to claim for many a church and an institution the prestige of having been founded by the apostles or their immediate disciples. What is certain is that already by the year 190 there was in Alexandria a center of Christian studies. It was there that Clement of Alexandria, an Athenian who was traveling from city to city in his quest for truth, met the teacher Pantenus, who taught him "the true philosophy"—that is, Christianity. Clement remained in Alexandria, where he succeeded Pantenus in the leadership of the school that the latter seems to have founded. There his most remarkable disciple was Origen, whom Bishop Demetrius put in charge of the training of catechumens—that is, candidates for baptism.

Although Origen's task was originally the preparation of the catechumens, his school soon became a center of Christian studies for those wishing to know more about their faith and even for pagans attracted by Origen's fame. Thus, for instance, Julia Mammea, the mother of Emperor Alexander Severus, went to hear the lectures of Origen. Besides theological subjects, the school taught sciences, mathematics, and other disciplines. In addition, occasionally some of its teachers were invited to places where there was a theological disagreement or concern, in order to help resolve the matter. Such was the case of Origen himself, who was invited to go to Arabia in order to settle some debates regarding the nature of God.

All of this means that, even though there were some similarities between the school of Alexandria and our modern seminaries, it was different in that its main purpose was not to prepare pastors but rather to study, clarify, and explore the Christian faith. But even so, there were remarkable leaders who studied in it. One of these was Gregory the Wonderworker, a disciple of Origen who eventually became bishop as well as an effective evangelist in the city of Neocaesarea, in Pontus. (According to one of his biographers, when Gregory became bishop of Neocaesarea there were seventeen Christians in the city, and when he died only seventeen pagans remained.) Little by little, the school in Alexandria became a center of studies where many leaders of the church were formed. We also know that at roughly the same time there was a similar school in Antioch. The most famous teacher of that other school was Lucian of Antioch, who taught Arius as well as most of his followers—who therefore called themselves "fellow Lucianists."

But one must remember that in order to be a pastor or a bishop the first requirement was to be elected by the congregation. Thus, although many of those who studied in these schools did eventually become pastors or bishops, they did not attend those schools as candidates for the ordained ministry but simply as people interested in Christian truth.

In summary, during the first centuries in the life of the church there were no formal programs of study for the pastorate. Since pastoral duties—particularly leading worship and teaching—required the ability to read and to interpret texts, it was common to elect as bishops those who had a measure of education—although usually that education had not been imparted by a school in the church but rather by the pagan system of education. Normally these studies were mostly in the fields of literature and its interpretation and rhetoric. Therefore, as we shall see, the distinction that we make between theological education for the church as a whole and the training for the pastorate did not exist in the early church.

As the distinction between bishops and presbyters developed, the former began supervising the latter not only in their pastoral practice but also in their theological education. Since soon it became customary to elect bishops from among presbyters, this resulted in a process of mentoring in which bishops trained their presbyters, and eventually their successors would be elected from among those whom they had trained.

As for Christian schools, these emerged in the second century but became much stronger in the third. Their specific purpose was not the training of ministers but the inquiring into and defense of the faith and catechetical instruction. But even so, soon there were alumni from the main schools—particularly those in Alexandria and Antioch—who did become bishops.

2
The Catechumenate

Although in the previous chapter reference was already made to the catechetical school of Alexandria, it is important to clarify the meaning of the word "catechetical," since for several centuries theological education—that is, the education of the entire community of believers—took place in two particular settings, the Service of the Word, of which we have already spoken, and the catechumenate.

The word "catechumenate" comes from "catechesis," which means teaching and may be found already in the Epistle to the Galatians 6:6: "Those who are taught the word [in Greek, *ho katēchoumenos*; and in the Latin Vulgate, *is qui catechizatur*] must share in all good things with their teacher [in Greek, *tō katēchounti*; and in the Vulgate, *ei qui se catechizat*]." And the same verb appears in Luke 1:4, where Luke refers to those things about which Theophilus has been "instructed" (catechized); in 1 Corinthians 14:19, where Paul declares that he would rather teach (catechize) than speak in tongues; and in Acts 18:25, where we are told that Apollos was "instructed [catechized] in the Way of the Lord" by Priscilla and Aquila.

The first converts to Christianity were either Jews or "God fearers"—that is, people who, like Cornelius and the Ethiopian eunuch, knew the faith of Israel, believed in the one God, and followed the moral principles of Israel, but for some reason did not become Jews. When such people accepted Jesus as the Messiah, they did not have to be instructed on those moral principles of the Judeo-Christian tradition, on the need to avoid idolatry, on the history of Israel, or on other similar matters. They already knew all that and practiced much of what was required of them. Therefore, they could be immediately baptized, as we see happening in Jerusalem in the early chapters of the book of Acts, as well as on the road to Gaza in the case of the Ethiopian eunuch and in Caesarea with Cornelius and his household. Certainly, accepting Christ was not an easy or unimportant matter, for it might also bring difficulties with the more traditional Jews, but the changes that were required, both in life and in beliefs, were not drastic.

As the new faith began making its way into circles that did not know the religion of Israel, nor the moral demands of the God of Israel and of the church, it became necessary to develop means to make certain that anyone who was baptized understood what was taking place and had already practiced the Christian way of life for a certain time, so as to know by experience what was required of believers, as well as the difficulties to be faced in society at large by the mere fact of being a Christian and belonging to the church. It was this need that resulted in the catechumenate.

It is not possible to say exactly when the catechumenate emerged. Toward the middle of the second century, Justin Martyr declared in his *First Apology* that

> as many as are persuaded and believe that what we teach and say is true, and undertake to be able to live accordingly, are instructed to pray and to entreat God with fasting, for the remission of sins that are past, we praying and fasting with them. Then they are brought to us where there is water, and are regenerated in the same manner in which we were ourselves regenerated. For, in the name of God, the Father and Lord of the universe, and of our Saviour Jesus Christ, and of the Holy Spirit, they then receive the washing with water.[1]

Justin gives no more details. But what he says is similar to what we know about the practices of the catechumenate a few decades later: a period of preparation, the support and solidarity of the rest of the church, and finally baptism itself. Yet the lack of details does not allow us to determine to what extent the catechumenate had developed in Justin's time into what it eventually became: a system of preparation for baptism that might take two or more years.

At the closing of the second century, Tertullian distinguished between orthodox Christians and heretics, among other things by declaring that among the heretics "it is doubtful who is a catechumen, and who a believer; they have access [to Communion] alike, they hear alike, they pray alike."[2] The distinction whose value Tertullian asserts, and apparently lacking among heretics, was part of the institution of the catechumenate. If someone expressed the wish to become a Christian and join the church, that person was asked to give proof of a firmness of purpose. Once such proof was given to the satisfaction of the bishop—which might take some time—the person was included among the *audientes*, that is, the hearers or listeners—something similar to what today some church reports and sociologists call "adherents" or "sympathizers." Such people could and should attend the Service of the Word, but at the beginning of the Service of the Table—that is, of Communion—they were dismissed.

When *audientes* had shown the seriousness of their purpose through a righteous life and perseverance in attending church and listening to the word, they were included among the "catechumens." Admission into the catechumenate was a formal step, marked with a number of rites that included the signing of the cross on the person's forehead. (At least in some churches, hands were imposed on the new catechumens, and a pinch of salt on which an exorcism had been pronounced was placed in their mouths.) Once declared part of the catechumenate, such people did not leave the Service of the Word when the *audientes* were dismissed, but remained for a special prayer on their behalf. They were then dismissed, still before the celebration of Communion.

The catechumenate was a period of instruction, doctrinal as well as moral and liturgical. At the beginning of that process the emphasis lay on moral practices and faithfulness to the Lord. What was underscored was the practice of the Christian life and the need to be faithful in the face of the many social pressures exerted against Christians, as well as under the threat of persecution, which was always a possibility.

The duration of the catechumenate varied. In 305, the acts of the Council of Elvira—a city now in ruins, near Granada, Spain—speak of two years, and the same duration appears in other ancient sources. If during that period someone proved to be unready or unworthy to receive baptism, the catechumenate could be prolonged significantly more—or the person could be restored to the rank of the *audientes* until signs were given of being ready to reinitiate the catechumenate. As we shall see, after the conversion of Constantine, when the catechumenate began to lose importance, it also became shorter. But before that time the most common duration was two years, and often three.

When the catechumens completed their period of preparation, they were included among the *competentes*—or, in Greek-speaking churches, the *phōtizomenoi*, that is, those who were in the process of illumination, for baptism was often spoken of as the enlightening of believers, or their receiving the light of the word.

The *competentes* then went through a period of special and intense preparation before receiving baptism. Since baptism was normally administered on Easter, that final period of special preparation in which—as Justin had noted much earlier—the entire church prayed and fasted for them, is the origin of Lent. During that period, the instruction included doctrinal matters, as well as the elements of the liturgy and the practice of a strict religious discipline. As we have seen, Justin declared that fasting and prayer were part of that period of preparation. But other authors also speak of being silent and practicing abstinence both in sexual matters and in food. As to the liturgy, all that was explained to them was

11

what was necessary to understand something of the baptismal rites in which they were to participate.[3] On the matter of doctrine, we fortunately have several documents that help us understand the contents of these instructions. Among them the most important is the *Catechesis* of Cyril of Jerusalem. The *Catechesis*—also known as *Catechetical Lectures*—of Cyril is composed of twenty-three lectures. The first eighteen are addressed to the *competentes*, or *phōtizomenoi*, in preparation for their baptism. The other five are more detailed explanations of the sacraments, particularly of Communion. The most interesting feature of these lectures is that they show to what extent it was thought that the teachings of the church were too important to be imparted to just anyone. The lectures begin with a clear indication of who the audience is: "You are already surrounded by an odor of joy, you who will soon be enlightened."[4] And then, toward the end of the prologue, Cyril includes the following warning:

> You may give these lectures for those who are to be enlightened, to candidates for baptism, and to those who are already baptized, so that they may read them. But if you spread them wide, or give them to catechumens, or to any who are not Christians, you will be responsible before to the Lord. And if you make a copy, include this warning at the beginning, as in the presence of the Lord.[5]

At least in some churches, the *competentes* then underwent a series of seven "scrutinies," which took place before the congregation of those already baptized. In the first scrutiny, the *competentes* gave their names. In each of them they were asked certain questions, and they were given some instructions. The third special scrutiny included instruction, among other things, on the Creed—of which there were different versions in various churches—the Lord's Prayer, and several other aspects of Christian doctrine.[6] The last scrutiny took place on Holy Saturday, and it was part of the rites through which a *competent* finally became one of the "faithful."

This is not the place to describe or discuss all these rites. Suffice it to say that they included the "renunciations," in which the neophyte—turning to the west, the realm of darkness—officially rejected Satan as well as the world and its pomp, and then—turning to the east—received Jesus Christ, the Sun of Righteousness. After the baptism itself, there were other rites such as anointing with oil, being dressed in a white robe, and finally participating for the first time in Communion, jointly with the rest of the congregation.

Even then the process of initiation and teaching of these neophytes continued, for they were now called "infants," for one more week. Finally, on the Sunday after Easter, they set aside the white robes of recently born Christians and received a final instruction about the rites through which they had passed. (That it is why even today some churches include in their Easter service the words of 1 Peter 2:2: "Like newborn infants, long for the pure, spiritual milk.") Among the many sermons of Augustine we have the following words about baptism and Communion, pronounced on in the night after Easter, and addressed to the neophytes who were now becoming full-fledged members of the church:

> In this loaf of bread you are given clearly to understand how much you should love unity. I mean, was that loaf made from one grain? Weren't there many grains of wheat? But before they came into the loaf they were all separate; they were joined together by means of water after a certain amount of pounding and crushing. Unless wheat is ground, after all, and moistened with water, it can't possibly get into this shape which is called bread. [Augustine then refers to the long period of preparation for baptism as a time of pounding and crushing. He continues:] ... Then came baptism, and you were, in a manner of speaking, moistened with water in order to be shaped into bread. But it's not yet bread without fire to bake it. ... So the Holy Spirit comes, fire after water, and you are baked into the bread which is the body of Christ. And that is how unity is signified.[7]
>
> In order not to be scattered and separated, eat what binds you together; in order not to seem cheap in your own estimation, drink the price that was paid for you. Just as this turns into you when you eat and drink it, so you for your part turn into the body of Christ when you live devout and obedient lives ... so you are beginning to receive what you have also begun to be.[8]

This "beginning to be" was the culmination of the catechetical process, now crowned with baptism but still requiring further growth into the fullness of the faith—a growth that would take place in the actual practice of the faith in daily life and in the constant study of scripture by continued attendance at the Service of the Word. But now the newly baptized, fully grafted into the body of Christ, were allowed to partake of Communion; and as part of the priestly people of God they were also allowed to participate in the "prayers of the people."

The reason why I have dwelt at length on this catechetical process is that, as far as we know, this was the only formal theological education that was required of pastors, and it was also required of every believer. No further studies were required for ordination—although there is no doubt that most of those who were elected to serve as ordained ministers had continued studying in the years between their baptism and their ordination.

Apart from such personal study, the only setting in which biblical, theological, and practical instruction took place was the Service of the Word that each Sunday preceded the Service of the Table. The Service of the Word had a strong educational emphasis and is the origin of our present-day sermons. On this point it is important to remember that in those times when there was no printing press most of the members of the church had no other way of reading or learning about scripture than when it was read out loud in the Service of the Word. It was there that they learned all that they knew of the Bible and where the pastor helped them understand what the biblical texts implied for their lives and their faith.

In summary, in the ancient church there was no difference between the biblical and theological training that the laity received and that which was required for ordination. Certainly, those who were ordained then had to continue studying in order to be able to lead in the Service of the Word, to train the new catechumens, and so forth. But as preparation for ordination itself, they were not required to know anything more than what the rest of the congregation knew—although, as was indicated earlier, in many cases those who were elected to be pastors had previously studied subjects such as rhetoric or philosophy.

3

From Constantine to the Germanic Invasions

On the matter of theology and theological studies, Constantine's conversion had two consequences that may at first seem contradictory. On the one hand, the hundred years immediately following that event produced some of the greatest theologians and writers of the entire history of the church: Athanasius, Eusebius of Caesarea, Basil the Great, John Chrysostom, Jerome, Ambrose, Augustine, and many others. But on the other hand the same years mark the time when the catechumenate began to decline.

The decline of the catechumenate began shortly after the conversion of Constantine. For some time, the ancient practices were continued. Some of the texts quoted earlier—for instance, from Cyril of Jerusalem and Augustine—date from that period shortly after Constantine. But by the year 506, two hundred years after the Synod of Elvira ordered that the catechumenate should last two years, another council gathered in Agder, in the south of what is now France, and limited that period to eighty days. And less than a century later Pope Gregory the Great reduced it even further to forty days.

There were two main reasons for this. The first was the increasing support that Constantine and most of his successors gave the church. This led to an explosion in the number of people asking to join the church by baptism. This growth was so rapid that the church was unable to find enough teachers and mentors to take responsibility for the catechetical instruction of the multitudes seeking baptism. People were baptized before being catechized, in the hope that by being part of the church they would learn the essentials of Christian faith and life. Also, before the time of Constantine most catechetical instruction was devoted to preparing candidates to live as Christians in a socially hostile atmosphere. After Constantine, that hostility rapidly waned, and it would then seem that a prolonged period of catechumenate was no longer necessary in order to resist the pressures of society. (To what point was society becoming more Christian and to what point was Christianity adapting to the customs and values of society at large is a subject of great importance but far beyond the scope of this book.)

The second reason leading to the decline of the catechetical system began late in the fourth century and reached its high point early in the fifth. This was the Germanic invasions. In a few years, the western portion of the ancient Roman Empire was invaded and conquered by Franks, Goths, Vandals, and many other Germanic peoples who until then had remained beyond the borders of the Rhine and the Danube. The very city of Rome was conquered by the Goths in 410. Twenty years later, when Augustine was about to die, the Vandals had traversed all of Western Europe and crossed the Strait of Gibraltar and were at the very gates of the city of Hippo in North Africa, where Augustine lived. Everywhere Roman institutions were disappearing—or at least were being transformed radically under the impact of Germanic cultures. Slightly before that time Ulfilas had reduced the language of the Goths to writing and had translated the Bible into that language, but most of the Germanic peoples had no written language. And even within those nations that had such an advantage, there were very few who were able to read.

Within the confines of ancient Roman Christianity, the Germanic conquerors rapidly converted to Christianity. But these conversions were so numerous and so rapid—and the new converts so lacking in disciplines of study—that the catechumenate either disappeared or was reduced to a minimum, requiring only that candidates for baptism know the Lord's Prayer and a few other rudiments of the faith. In some of the borderlands of the ancient Roman Empire—that is, in missionary lands—there remained a formal catechumenate for pagans who were converted. But, since many of these conversions took place in mass and often under military coercion, even there the catechumenate was reduced to a minimum.

Furthermore, now a radical change took place in the manner in which both baptism and Communion were understood. As to baptism, as early as the time of Tertullian it had begun to be seen as a washing away of all previously committed sins, and therefore there was a tendency among some to postpone it as much as possible, or at least until one had left behind the sins of youth—a practice which Tertullian recommended.[1] Likewise, rulers and other public figures frequently postponed baptism for fear that their civil and legal responsibilities would clash with their duty as baptized Christians. This is why Emperor Constantine himself was not baptized until he was on his deathbed. For the same reason Ambrose, even though he had embraced the Christian faith since childhood, did not receive

16

baptism until he had already been elected bishop. But at the same time there was the opposite tendency, which rapidly made the baptism of infants normative. Both tendencies were based on the same vision of baptism as a washing away of all sins committed before the sacred rite took place. Since now there seemed to be no opposition between the church and society at large, baptism, which until that time had been a sign marking a select group of people who were ready to face many social and legal pressures, now became a sign of being a full participant in society at large. To this were added notions of original sin whose consequence was that those who died without being baptized supposedly could not go to heaven. This was one of the reasons why the practice of baptizing infants prevailed. We know that from much earlier—at least from the middle of the second century—it was customary to baptize infants; but these were children of Christian parents and were often baptized jointly with the rest of their families. Now it was expected that every child should be baptized as soon as possible—with the exception of Jews who converted to Christianity, who had to go through a period of preparation before being baptized. The decisions shortening the period of preparation for baptism, which have already been mentioned, first to eighty days and then to forty, were actually directed mostly at Jews who converted to Christianity and who were now practically the only ones who were baptized as adults—except for the various Germanic peoples, whose mass conversions continued for centuries.

However, as already stated, this period in which the catechumenate was declining also produced some of the greatest writers and thinkers in the entire history of Christianity. In the Latin-speaking West, there are three figures who deserve particular attention as mentors through whom medieval Christianity was able to receive a measure of the knowledge and the letters of antiquity: Ambrose (339–97), Jerome (ca. 342–420), and Augustine (354–430). These three lived at the dusk of the ancient Western Roman Empire. They, as well as others of less renown, were the bridge that connected the Western medieval church with antiquity, both Christian and Greco-Roman.

In 378, four years after Ambrose was made bishop of Milan, the Visigoths defeated and killed Emperor Valens in the battle of Adrianapolis. After reaching the very walls of Constantinople, they turned westward, and their depredations continued until they were allowed to settle in the region of Moesia. This invasion was followed by many others, eventually leading to the fall of Rome and to the end of the Western Roman Empire. The result was the loss of much of classical literature, to the point that very soon it was almost only the clergy who knew how to read. This in turn led several of the most distinguished ecclesiastical lead-ers of the following centuries to write a series of works for the instruction of the clergy, who knew little of classical letters. One of the first of these writings was the three books of Ambrose, *On the Duties of the Clergy*, whose Latin title, *De of-ficiis ministrorum*, shows that it was patterned after Cicero's *De officiis*, expanding, correcting, and adapting it to the specific case of the clergy. Ambrose's purpose in writing this work was that it would serve as an instrument for the instruction of the clergy, as he himself says:

> And I am speaking of the duties which I wish to impress upon and impart to you, whom I have chosen for the service of the Lord; so that those things which have been already implanted and fixed in your minds and characters by habit and training may now be further unfolded to you by explanation and instruction.[2]

Ambrose himself had been born and raised before the beginning of the de-bacle. By the time he was elected to be a bishop he had received a solid education as preparation for the career in administration and public service that lay ahead of him. It was only after his ordination that, as already stated, he began theologi-cal studies under the direction of his mentor Simplician. As he himself declares: "I was carried off . . . to enter on the priesthood, and began to teach you, what I myself had not yet learnt. So it happened that I began to teach before I began to learn."[3]

For Ambrose this is not an obstacle but rather leads him to an interesting pedagogical observation that "in the endeavour to teach, I may be able to learn."[4]

If Ambrose lived in a time when the threat and penetration into the Empire by Germanic tribes was increasing, Jerome was able to witness that threat becom-ing reality. In the year 410 the Goths, under the command of Alaric, took and sacked the city of Rome. The unbelievable news reached Jerome in his retirement in Bethlehem, where he declared: "Who would believe that Rome, built up by the conquest of the whole world, has collapsed, that the mother of all nations has become also their tomb?"[5] "The City which had taken the whole world was itself taken."[6] But, even without knowing it, Jerome himself was opening the way for the intellectual life of the coming Middle Ages in at least two directions.

The first of these two directions was the use of monastic life for study and scholarship. With few exceptions, until then the main purpose of monasticism had been the ascetic life. Without forsaking that ascetic dimension of monasti-cism, Jerome turned his retreat in Bethlehem into an opportunity for study and writing and particularly of the study of scripture. In that task his main collabora-tors were Paula and her daughter Eustoquium, who studied biblical languages with him and then collaborated with him in the production of the Vulgate.

18

Therefore the lives themselves of Jerome, Paula, and Eustoquium show that monasticism was becoming a means for studying—and this would become one of its main contributions during the Middle Ages.

The second direction in which Jerome opened the way for medieval Christianity was the Vulgate itself, that is, the translation of the Bible into common or "vulgar" Latin. Jerome was a literary genius, and this allowed him to translate the sacred text to a Latin that, while reflecting the use of the language in his time, was also elegant and polished. At the beginning there was strong resistance to this new translation on the part of those who preferred the older but less elegant *Vetus Latina*, but in the end the quality and elegance of the Vulgate prevailed. The Psalms in the Vulgate, which Jerome had repeatedly revised and corrected, bore the mark of genius, combining the beauty of classical Latin poetry with the actual language of the people. They soon became the Psalter that medieval monastics recited or sang in their hours of devotion and that most of the laity also came to know by heart.

Augustine, who was some ten years younger that Jerome, also died some ten years later, when the invading Vandals were at the very gates of his city of Hippo. Therefore, if the sack of Rome in 410 marks the decline of classical antiquity, the day of Augustine's death in 430 may be said to mark the death of that antiquity.

Like Jerome, Augustine left for his successors in the Middle Ages the double legacy of a monastic life devoted to study and a vast literary production through which the Middle Ages were able to know something of the culture and letters of antiquity.

As to monastic life, Augustine's ideal between the time of his conversion in Milan and his ordination as a presbyter in Hippo was a life of tranquil devotion and study surrounded by a number of friends of similar inclinations who would live in simplicity and sharing all, as in the monastic tradition, but without the extreme asceticism of some monks. After his conversion, and before he was baptized, Augustine began practicing this by withdrawing with a few friends, his mother Monica, and his son Adeodatus to a villa that a friend had in Cassiciacum, near Milan. Later, upon returning to his native Africa, he established a community of study and devotion in Tagaste. When, in one of his outings from that community, he visited the city of Hippo, Valerius, the local bishop, forced him to accept ordination. Augustine agreed only if he would be allowed to live in Hippo in a community similar to the one he had founded in Tagaste. That community was the origin and inspiration of what later became known as the "Canons of Saint Augustine"—among whom, more than a thousand years later, Martin Luther would be trained. Therefore, like Jerome, Augustine turned the monastic life into an occasion for study and scholarship. But, since his canons in Hippo were those who also collaborated with him in the ministerial tasks, this monastic life turned study into a means of preparing for those tasks. Thus, one can say that those canons that Augustine gathered around himself in Hippo were the precursors of the monastic schools that soon would come to have an important place in the task of theological education.

The literary work of Saint Augustine is so vast that it is quite impossible to summarize it in a few paragraphs. However, a few words must be said about three works that were among the most studied in the Middle Ages—*The City of God*, the *Enchiridion*, and *On Christian Doctrine*—in order then to direct our attention to the treatise in which Augustine deals specifically with the matter of teaching and learning, *De magistro—On the teacher*.

The City of God is an extensive defense of Christian faith against those who claimed that the fall of Rome was due to the abandonment of the ancient gods in favor of Christianity. But the book is much more than that, because in order to refute such opinions Augustine offers an entire philosophy of history. Furthermore, in expounding that philosophy of history he tells of events, retells ancient myths and stories, offers geographic descriptions, and quotes authors who otherwise would have been forgotten during the Middle Ages.

The purpose of the *Enchiridion* is not entirely clear. Augustine wrote it in response to a certain Laurentius, who lived in Rome in about 420—that is, ten years after the sack of the city by the Goths. But this short compendium of the Christian faith soon became one of the most read and studied writings in late antiquity, and remained so for most medieval clergy, for it summarizes the very essence of Christian doctrine and its relationship with both morality and reason.

However, Augustine's *On Christian Doctrine* was more influential among medieval clergy than the two works previously cited. This was a relatively short handbook, but very complete, and therefore it became the main textbook for many medieval clergymen who needed a brief introduction and explanation of the main doctrines of Christianity. In the prologue of this work, Augustine shows that its purpose is didactic and that his hope is that the book will serve as a teacher of teachers, that is, as a book instructing the clergy: "There are certain rules for the interpretation of Scripture. I believe that such rules can easily be taught to those devoted to the study of Scripture, so that not only they will profit by reading those authors who discerned the secrets of Scripture, but also by their teaching they can be of benefit to others."[7]

But Augustine is quite conscious that—in his time as well as in ours—there are those who claim to have a special understanding of scriptures without having been taught:

> As for those who claim to have a special gift from God and boast of being able to understand and teach the sacred books without the rules that I will deliver here...let

20

them remember that even their first letters they learned with the help of others....If he can read and understand without any need of human teaching, why does he try to teach others, rather than simply directing them to God, who will teach them directly as God [supposedly] did for them?[8]

This work came to be the fountain from which later generations drank, particularly in the early centuries of the Middle Ages. It was therefore the main textbook that many employed as the basic manual in ministerial training.

The treatise *De magistro* was written by Augustine in 389, only two years after his own baptism, and it was less read during the Middle Ages than the previously mentioned works. But in it Augustine expresses how he understands teaching, and that understanding of the teacher's task, which appears repeatedly in his other writings, prevailed in Western Christianity at least until the thirteenth century. The treatise itself takes the form of a dialogue between Augustine and his son Adeodatus. After a detailed discussion on the function of words as signs and on the relationship between the significant and the signified, Adeodatus comes to the conclusion that

all we can learn through words are words, or rather, their sound and noise....For we do not learn the words that we already know, and we cannot claim to have learned those we do not know in any other way than by understanding their meaning, which does not come to us by hearing the words, but rather by the knowledge of those things they signify....When words are pronounced, we either know or do not know their meaning. If we do know it, rather than learning we are remembering. And if we do not know it, we do not even remember, but are simply invited to seek for the meaning of the words.[9]

This in turn means that

we come to understand the many things that come into our mind, not by consulting the outer voice [of the teacher] that speaks to us, but rather by the inner consideration of the truth that reigns in the spirit....And this truth that teaches and is to be considered is Christ.[10]

All of this leads to the conclusion that a human teacher does not really teach but only helps the learner to discover and recognize what the word of God has already placed in the learner's mind. The function of the teacher is limited to helping the disciple to discover the truth that, while present in the mind, is not acknowledged or has been forgotten. This is a Christian version of the ancient maieutic of Socrates, in which the function of the teacher is like that of a midwife who helps the soul to bring forth what is already in it. In this Christian version, this leads to joining learning and contemplation so closely that the two cannot be separated. One comes to know the unknown, not through investigation based on observation but rather through a contemplative and virtuous life, which in turn helps the learner to see more clearly the word of God that is already within. Therefore, according to Augustine, the function of a Christian teacher is not so much to instruct as to guide—to guide disciples to the truth that is already in them by virtue of the presence of the eternal Word in the human mind.

In summary, the period immediately following the conversion of Constantine, and up to the Germanic invasions, saw a multitude of great Christian teachers but also was a period of decline for the catechumenate, which almost disappeared and continued being employed only among converted Jews and new Christians in missionary territories.

But during the same time the practice also arose of employing monastic life as an opportunity to study. This would herald the monastic schools that soon came to occupy a central place in the intellectual life of Europe, as well as in preparation for ministry.

It is also important to note that during this period several authors emerged who, even without proposing to do so, for they had no idea what the future would bring, would become the main sources through which the Middle Ages would drink from the theological waters of Christian antiquity. Among these, the most significant are Jerome's Vulgate, Ambrose's treatise *On the Duties of the Clergy*, and Augustine's *On Christian Doctrine*.

Lastly, one must take note that, even though the schools in Alexandria and Antioch continued to exist, there were still no schools for the preparation of ministers. Some bishops—notably Saint Augustine, but also many others—gathered around themselves associates who, while serving as collaborators with the bishops, were also mentored by them.

4
The Romanization of the Germanic Peoples

The purpose of the Germanic peoples for invading Roman territories was not to destroy the Empire and its civilization but rather to take possession of its wealth as well as of its traditions and institutions. As a result, the conquerors progressively adopted the religion and most of the customs of the conquered. The various languages of the invaders, besides not having been reduced to writing, were sufficiently different among themselves so as to make communication difficult, and therefore Latin soon was restored as the means of communication among various peoples, even though in fact it was not their mother tongue. For these reasons, in the recently emerged Germanic kingdoms the administration was in the hands of a Latin-speaking bureaucracy, many of whom were clergy. Thus Latin remained the common language among the educated in Western Christendom, and this in turn helped new generations of clergy to study the writings of Christian antiquity—writings such as those of Ambrose, Jerome, and Augustine.

It is most important to remember that the main Roman institution that continued after the Germanic invasions was the church. Due to the need to read and explain the word, those who knew how to read and had a certain measure of education were clergy. For this reason the clergy now were responsible not only for presiding worship and expounding scripture but also for teaching the new generations, as well as counseling kings and other political leaders, managing the business and policies of entire kingdoms, and other similar tasks. But such tasks were reserved for the better-educated clergy, while those who often practiced the pastorate, particularly in rural and poor areas, had little or no formal education.

In general, the ignorance of the clergy was abysmal. If they appeared to be educated, this was due to the contrast between them and the warlike and illiterate conquerors. In order to respond to this situation, some studious Christians wrote books whose purpose was to instruct the clergy. Among them one may mention Magnus Aurelius Cassiodorus and Isidore of Seville, but above all Pope Gregory the Great.

Cassiodorus was born slightly more than a half century after the death of Augustine and lived from approximately 485 to about 580. He came from a family from southern Italy that for seven generations had held important public offices. He followed the same route, first at the service of the Byzantine Empire in the city of Ravenna, and then serving the Visigothic King Theodoric—which is an indication of the important role that the conquered Romans had in the administration of the new Germanic kingdoms. During the reign of Theodoric there was a brief awakening in the study of letters, and it was precisely at that time and under those circumstances that Cassiodorus lived. While busy in his administrative and diplomatic tasks, Cassiodorus was also concerned over the poor state of letters in his time and was convinced of the need to educate the clergy. To that end he proposed to Pope Agapitus that a school be founded in Rome, but various military and political vicissitudes made this impossible. Eventually, Cassiodorus founded a monastery in Vivarium, the land of his ancestors, and withdrew to it. As he himself describes the purpose of this foundation, he intended it to become like a city whose inhabitants would not have to worry about the occupations of daily life but rather devote themselves to the worship of God and to studying and copying books. Once again we see how, as letters declined among the rest of the population, monastic life tended to be a refuge where ancient knowledge was preserved.

Although it was thanks to the monks in Vivarium that many of the writings of antiquity were preserved, the main contribution of Cassiodorus was through his book *Institutions of Divine and Secular Letters—Institutiones Divinarum et Saecularium Litterarum—*which was addressed to clergy wishing to improve their education and also sought to encourage them to further studies. One may note that in this book Cassiodorus changed the meaning of the traditional term "liberal arts." In earlier antiquity a distinction had been made between the "liberal arts" and the "servile arts." The latter were the tasks reserved for serfs or slave (*servi*), while the former were accessible to those who were free (*liberi*). But according to Cassiodorus, the word *liberalis* comes from *liber*, book, and therefore this term does not refer to tasks or occupations that are higher in the social scale but rather to those having to do with books. Thus, even though Cassiodorus wanted the monks in Vivarium to have the leisure to devote themselves to the liberal arts, he did not wish this to be understood in the sense that the liberal arts were higher than those that were traditionally deemed "servile."

As their title indicates, the *Institutions* of Cassiodorus deal with what he calls "secular letters" as well as with those that he calls "divine"—that is, both with classical studies and with Bible and theology. In reverse order to what later became normative, the first part of this work is devoted to theological matters, and the "liberal arts" occupy its latter part. There is no doubt that the purpose of Cassiodorus in writing this book was to instruct both the monks in Vivarium and the clergy at large. This is why at the beginning he includes an extensive bibliography of readings recommended for the study of the "divine letters." There is every indication that this bibliography was in fact a catalog of the books available in Vivarium. In any case, there is no doubt that what Cassiodorus wanted to accomplish with the entire writing as well as with his bibliography was to establish a program of studies for ecclesiastical leaders. In that program, he reaffirmed the traditional curriculum of classical letters, in which, after the very first studies where one learned to read, write, and sing Psalms, studies were divided into two sections: the *trivium*—that is, the three main roads (which, by the way, is the origin of our word *trivial*). Traditionally these three arts or fields of knowledge were grammar, astronomy, and rhetoric. But by now the study of these three arts was mostly directed to ministerial and pastoral tasks. Thus, grammar was understood in a wider sense than it is today, for it included also an introduction to classical and patristic writings, as well as principles for the interpretation of those writings and of scripture. Astronomy was employed mostly to determine the feasts and various observances in the religious calendar. And rhetoric was directed to preaching and teaching. The *trivium* was followed by the *quadrivium*—that is, the "four ways"—which included logic, arithmetic, geometry, and music. And then, on the basis of this knowledge, one would turn to the field of "scripture"— which actually included all theological studies—as well as some practical aspects of pastoral tasks.

Isidore of Seville was born around 560 and died in 636. Thus, he was some twenty years old when Cassiodorus died. One of his admiring contemporaries tells us about the harsh times in which it was his lot to live and the importance of his work in such times: "This man was raised by God in the difficult times through which we are living in Hispania after so many catastrophes, as I believe, in order to restore the teachings and witnesses of the ancients. So that we will not become hardened in an atmosphere of ignorance, but praise him as a sort of tutor for us."[1]

Like Cassiodorus before him, Isidore sought to link all study and knowledge. The clear intention of his work was to contribute to the formation of the Spanish clergy. For this reason he dealt with every conceivable subject in heaven as well as on earth, for his vision was that there be a clergy learned not only in Bible and theology but in every field of knowledge. His work is a true encyclopedia of the knowledge of his time, including subjects such as "On Ecclesiastical Books and Functions" (book vi), "On God, the Angels, and the Faithful" (book vii), and "On the Church and the Sects" (book viii) but also, among other subjects, grammar (book i), rhetoric and dialectic (book ii), mathematics (book iii), medicine (book iv), and an enormous variety of similar subjects. Although this Isidorian encyclopedia circulated first in Spain, it soon was known in the rest of medieval Europe, thus becoming one of the major sources through which Western Europe inherited much of the knowledge of antiquity.

However, the most significant work for the formation of clergy in the early centuries of the Middle Ages was the *Pastoral Rule* of Gregory the Great, who was bishop of Rome from 590 to 604. In contrast with the writings of Cassiodorus and Isidore, and much more like the work of Ambrose, Gregory's *Pastoral Rule* is sharply focused on the responsibilities of the clergy and how to fulfill them. At the very beginning of his work, Gregory complains that, in contrast with occupations such as medicine, in which those who have not studied the matter carefully do not dare engage, there are among the clergy many who dare to teach without having studied. Thus, in words that would find an echo today, he declares at the very beginning of his work that:

> No one claims to be able to teach an art until first having learned it through careful study. With what incredible boldness then do the unlearned and unskillful stand ready to assume pastoral authority, forgetting that the care of souls is the art of arts! For it is clear that the ills of the mind are more hidden than the ills of the bowels. And yet quite often those who have no knowledge whatever of spiritual principles dare to declare themselves physicians of the heart, while those who do not know of the use of drugs would never dare to call themselves physicians of the flesh![2]

But Gregory also declares that knowledge is not enough, for it must be accompanied by the practice of faith. Therefore, once again in words that would find echo today, he says that:

> Some take meticulous care in the study of spiritual principles, but what they achieve with their understanding they destroy with their lives. What they have learned through study and they now teach they do not practice. Thus what their words teach their conduct denies. And therefore it happens that the shepherds take risks at the cliffs, and the flock that follows falls into the abyss.[3]

Such statements are followed by several chapters outlining the main traits that pastors should have. For instance, they are to measure their words, on the one hand in order not to say anything that might lead to error and the other in order to avoid the possibility that, by being too often repeated, the truth they seek to teach may be weakened, "for quite often the power and effect on the hearts of those who hear are weakened by untimely abundance of words."[4] Likewise, the leaders of the flock are to combine firmness of purpose with humility, "so that just as they show their great authority outwardly, they will also limit it inwardly."[5]

Gregory turns then to the more practical and extensive part of his work, in which he gives advice on how to deal with various sorts of people, which he presents in marked contrast, so that the pastor will understand that his first task is to determine with what sort of person, vices, or virtues he is dealing. This can be seen in the very titles of various chapters, such as: "That the poor have to be admonished in one way, and the rich in another" (chapter ii); "That the worldly ones are to be admonished in one way, and the illiterate in another" (chapter vi); "That the fainthearted are to be admonished in one way, and the forward in another" (chapter viii); "That the feisty ones are to be admonished in one way and the slothful in another" (chapter xv); and so forth

Gregory's *Pastoral Rule* was one of the most widely read books throughout the Middle Ages, for it became the main textbook for most of the clergy—to which many added the works already mentioned by Ambrose, Augustine, Cassiodorus, Isidore, and others of lesser importance.

In summary, the greatest challenge that the early Middle Ages had to face concerning the training of clergy was the decline and almost disappearance of ancient letters, both secular and religious, from which earlier generations had benefitted—people such as Cyprian, Ambrose, and Augustine, who had been well educated before they reached the pastorate. Now, in the early Middle Ages, such an educational background was rarely available. In response to that situation, leaders in the church wrote a series of books that would be widely read during the Middle Ages. Some of these were encyclopedic in nature, such as the *Institutions* of Cassiodorus and the *Etymologies* of Isidore, and others were more directly practical, such as Ambrose's *Of the Duties of the Clergy* and the *Pastoral Rule* of Gregory. The principal means through which most of the clergy in the early Middle Ages were educated was the reading of such books, as well as by being mentored by other clergymen. However, there were also schools in which the first letters were taught, followed by the *trivium* and *quadrivium*, and in some cases by biblical and theological studies. It is to these schools that we must now turn our attention.

5
Early Medieval Schools

The Germanic invasions were just one of a long series of invasions that shook Western Europe during the early centuries of the Middle Ages. Practically at the same time as the Germanic peoples came, the Huns came. Then, in the seventh century, most of the Middle East and the entire northern coast of Africa was invaded and conquered by Arabs, and many converted to Islam. Early in the following century (711) the Moors crossed the Strait of Gibraltar, destroyed the Visigothic kingdom in Spain, and invaded France; finally, in 732, in the battle of Tours, or of Poitiers, they were stopped by the Franks under the leadership of Charles Martel. This allowed for a brief renaissance under the reign of the Carolingians—the descendants of Charles Martel. But this renaissance did not last long, and one of the reasons for its decline was the repeated invasions from Normans, followed by Slavs and Magyars, or Hungarians. The Normans were particularly destructive in that they sacked and destroyed monasteries—among them some of the most ancient and distinguished monasteries in Ireland, where much of the knowledge of antiquity had been preserved—thus bringing a new period of chaos and hostilities. (However, it is interesting that, once they were converted to Christianity, the Normans devoted themselves to founding and building monasteries with as much enthusiasm as they had earlier employed in destroying them.)

Under such conditions, all education, both religious and secular—if one is allowed to make such a distinction at a time when everything was viewed from a religious perspective—took place in two main and very influential institutions: monastic schools and cathedral schools.

As already stated, during the latter years of antiquity, under the leadership of leaders such as Jerome, Augustine, and many others, monastic life began to

29

tend toward study. At some time around the year 529, Saint Benedict of Nursia produced his famous *Rule*, which would shape most of Western monasticism to this day. The *Rule* said little about study—and what it said was mostly concerning the novitiate, the preparation for the hours of prayer, and spending most of Sunday reading.[1] But soon, due in part to the example of intellectuals such as Augustine and Jerome, many monastic houses, both male and female, began taking study quite seriously. In these houses—particularly those for males—schools were founded whose double purpose was to educate the children given to the monastery as "oblates" and to educate the children of the nobility who were preparing for careers in civil administration. It was thus that monastic schools came to be an essential part of the medieval educational system. Since monasteries also paid much attention to the copying of manuscripts, besides their important function as centers of study, they also became centers for the preservation and diffusion of the knowledge and letters of antiquity.

At first, as is clear in the Benedictine *Rule*, monasteries were not intended to be institutions for the training of ordained ministry, since it was expected that once a monk made permanent vows he would spend the rest of his days in that particular house and not move to another monastery nor become a parish priest. But even so, soon monasteries became centers producing pastors and prelates. This may be seen, for instance, in the case of Gregory the Great, who was forced by the pope to leave the monastery in order to devote himself to active ministry; he eventually became a pope himself. Something similar happened in the case of Augustine of Canterbury and his companions, whom Pope Gregory now took from the monastery in order to send them as missionaries to England. After that time, there were ever more frequent cases of monks who, either by their own decision or by command, left the monasteries in order to work actively in pastoral tasks or to occupy other ecclesiastical positions. Four centuries after Gregory's time, the Abbey of Bec, in Normandy, provided Lanfranc and Anselm to serve as archbishops of Canterbury, and one of its monks became first a bishop and then Pope Alexander II.

At an earlier time, the most basic form of theological education had been the catechetical system through which candidates prepared for baptism. Now its place was taken by the novitiate through which monks prepared for their final vows. Both the novitiate and the earlier catechetical system sought to provide people with the necessary theological instruction and character formation to join a community in which a particular and often difficult lifestyle would be expected from them: in the case of catechumens, the church; and, in the case of novices, the monastery. This was part of a radical change: what was earlier expected of most Christians and offered to them was now reserved for a smaller group of particularly devout Christians, the monastics. (Likewise, the earlier practice of sharing goods among all believers, now abandoned by the church at large, became a fundamental dimension of monastic life. And the task of praying for the entire world, as the priestly people of God, was now entrusted to monastic houses.)

The most outstanding monastic schools from the seventh century until the eleventh were those in Ireland. Since that island was set apart from the rest of Europe, most of the invasions that flooded all of the continent and Great Britain did not reach them—until the twelfth century, when the Normans invaded the island. Furthermore, the Irish church—traditionally said to have been founded by Saint Patrick—developed a system of government different from what was becoming common on the Continent and eventually in Great Britain. In Ireland, authority resided mostly in the abbots and abbesses of monasteries and convents, who also served as bishops or as supervisors of all ecclesiastical life. Also, since ancestral pagan times, there had been in Ireland the tradition of the bards, whose task was to compose poems in which the history of the land was told and celebrated and by means of which that history was taught to later generations. After the conversion of the land, that task of preserving the past and interpreting the present passed from the bards to the monasteries. For these reasons, Irish monasteries became centers of study and learning where ancient manuscripts were preserved and copied, where Greek continued being studied even when it had practically disappeared in the rest of Western Europe, and where people from both Great Britain and the Continent went to study. Although most of those monasteries had around fifty students, there were several that had more than a thousand, and at least a few of them reached the figure of three thousand students. As a result of the fame of the Irish schools and of the disorder prevalent elsewhere, the number of students from those other regions was such that one of them (Adelm of Sherborne) wrote a friend that these students arrived in "small fleets." The Venerable Bede, in his *Ecclesiastical History of England*, declares that in times when plague and chaos rule in England, "many nobility, and of the lower ranks of the English nation,... forsaking their native island, retired thither, either for the sake of Divine studies, or of a more continent life; and some of them presently devoted themselves to a monastical life, others chose rather to apply themselves to study, going about from one master's cell to another."[2]

Among the nobility who went to Ireland to study were three kings, two of Northumbria and one of France. But the most famous product of these schools was the Englishman Alcuin of York, whom we shall meet again when dealing with the policies and schools of the Carolingians. Irish monasteries also contributed to literature on the practice of ministry through an entire series of books known as "penitential books," or simply as "penitentials." It was in Ireland that private confession first came to take the place of the previous practice of public confession, and it was also there that the first manuals for confessors were produced. They contain practical and complete instructions on how to deal with all sorts of sin, evaluating them and determining what would be an appropriate penance—fasting, abstinence, pilgrimage, and so forth. The most ancient of the Irish penitentials that has been preserved is that of Finian, an Irish monk in the sixth century. Slightly later, but equally popular, was the penitential of Quinian, another Irish monk who seems to have written around the year 650. The practical and pastoral tone of these manuals may be seen in some of the dictates of Finian:

> 3. If anyone has thought evil and intended to do it, but opportunity has failed him, it is the same sin but not the same penalty; for example, if he intended fornication or murder, since the deed did not complete the intention he has, to be sure, sinned in his heart, but if he quickly does penance, he can be helped. This penance of his is half a year on an allowance, and he shall abstain from wine and meats for a whole year.[3]

> 10. But if one who is a cleric falls miserably through fornication he shall lose his place of honor, and if it happens once [only] and it is concealed from men but known before God, he shall do penance for an entire year with an allowance of bread and water and for two years abstain from wine and meats, but he shall not lose his clerical office. For, we say, sins are to be absolved in secret by penance and by very diligent devotion of heart and body.[4]

> 23. If any cleric commits murder and kills his neighbor..., he must become an exile for ten years... and having thus completed the ten years, if he has done well and is approved by testimonial of the abbot or priest to whom he was committed, he shall be received into his own country and make satisfaction to the friends of him whom he slew, and he shall render to his father or mother, if they are still in the flesh, compensation for the filial piety and obedience [of the murdered man] and say: "Lo, I will do for you whatever you ask, in the place of your son."[5]

These penitential books circulated widely all over Europe, where they served as manuals for confessors. Thus, monastic schools, particularly those in Ireland, not only preserved the knowledge of antiquity but also provided pastors with concrete guides for the practice of their ministry.

As to the cathedral schools, we have already seen that, at least from the time of Cyprian in the third century, and probably from a much earlier date, there were bishops who established programs of education and sometimes of examinations to be given to candidates for ordination, and that toward the end of the fourth century Augustine did something similar with his clergy. These practices eventually led to the creation of cathedral schools—that is, schools attached to cathedrals—that undertook the task of instructing prospective clergy and future civil servants. Given the prejudices typical of the times, all students in these schools were male, for women were not allowed to enter either of these two careers. At the same time, some of the Germanic people, particularly the Normans, brought with them the principles of primogeniture, according to which the eldest son was the sole heir of his father, thus usually leaving younger sons with little or no inheritance. As a result, a growing number of students in the cathedral schools, as well as in monasteries, were sons of the lower nobility whose elder brothers would inherit the land and titles of nobility, leaving for them only three possible paths: military life, in which they would seldom reach the higher ranks reserved for their elder brothers; the religious life of monks and priests; and civil administration.

Cathedral schools arose in different areas, apparently without any coordinated effort. We know that there were already such schools in Spain early in the sixth century, for they are mentioned in the acts of the Second Council of Toledo, in 527. Soon there were similar schools throughout Gaul and England. As has already been mentioned, at about the same time Cassiodorus intended to create such a school in Rome, but could not bring his plan to fruition. Soon the idea itself of cathedral schools expanded beyond the cities and their cathedrals to some town and rural parishes, where parochial schools emerged. We find instructions about such schools in the acts of the Third Council of Vaison, gathered in France in 529. Although it is impossible to know exactly what was taught in these parochial schools, apparently it was limited to the most basic education and to the central doctrines of the faith. There are also indications that some students would move from these rural schools to those in monasteries and cathedrals. (For instance, under the Carolingians, Bishop Theodulf of Orleans invited priests under his supervision to have their relatives follow such a course.)

The destruction of the Visigothic kingdom in Spain by the Moors in 711 led to the disappearance of many cathedral and monastic schools in the peninsula. In the rest of Europe, as well as in Great Britain, there was a similar decline, although not quite as marked. In the midst of that darkness, one should point out the significant work of Hilda, abbess of Whitby, who established in her convent two schools, one for boys and another for girls, with the purpose that both the clergy of the area and the nuns of Whitby be able to attain an excellent education not only in religion but also in Latin grammar and literature. Soon thereafter, during the regime of the Carolingians, and particularly of Charlemagne, there was a brief awakening of study and intellectual debate in what is today France and Germany. Charlemagne was very much interested in promoting study throughout his kingdom. He took several measures to that end. One of them was to bring Alcuin of York from England. Alcuin was a monk who had studied in the Irish monasteries and whom Charlemagne entrusted with the founding and the organization of a school at the imperial palace. Charlemagne himself studied there, as well as his wife, his sons and daughter, and several important persons in the life of the palace and in the administration of the kingdom.

Part of the project of Charlemagne and Alcuin was to produce copies both of scripture and of other writings of antiquity in order to distribute them among schools and monasteries. It is said that Charlemagne himself, overcome by the immensity of the task and enthused by what he had learned about Augustine and Jerome, complained that he did not have a dozen such people, and that Alcuin commented: "the Creator of heaven and earth has only two of them. And you ask for a dozen!"

Charlemagne's interest in education—particularly in the education of the clergy and of a cadre of managers to serve the state—may be seen in several documents of his time, as well as in the decisions and edicts of various ecclesiastical bodies. An example of this is the recommendation of the council gathered in Frankfort in 794 that every bishop should attend to the education of his clergy. In 789 Charlemagne proclaimed a *General Admonition* whose eighty-two articles included an entire program for the reformation of the clergy. Two years before that, he had asked Pope Hadrian the First to send him a collection of directives that could be used for that purpose, and now Charlemagne's *Admonition* took the papal answer and expanded it. By royal order, it was proclaimed throughout the Frankish kingdom. Soon thereafter, Charlemagne published an *Epistle on the Cultivation of Letters*, which clearly bears the mark of the interests and the style of Alcuin and which therefore many attribute to Alcuin himself. These documents established a general educational policy for all the lands under Charlemagne's rule. The emphasis was on the education of the clergy—and within that education, on biblical studies. Following the pattern that had long been established, Alcuin and Charlemagne proposed a program of studies in which, after the *trivium* and *quadrivium*, one would move on to biblical and theological studies. Thanks to the support of Charlemagne and to the relative peace that reigned at least in the heartland of his kingdom, the educational reforms that the king and his advisors proposed had great success, for soon there were more than thirty famous cathedral and monastic schools, as well as some other forty of less renown, and countless parochial schools.

As was to be expected, such studies led to theological controversies and debates that do not have to be discussed here—particularly since I have done so elsewhere.[6] But one should at least mention Hrabanus Maurus (776–856), a disciple of Alcuin who is most commonly studied for his theories on the Eucharist, predestination, and other subjects, but who also wrote an important treatise *De clericorum institutione*—*On the institutions of clerics*. This is part of the long list of books that we have already encountered whose purpose is the instruction of the clergy and other ecclesiastical leaders. In it, Hrabanus moves from the practical to the theoretical, for the first two books deal with subjects such as ministerial orders, vestments, sacraments, and liturgy, while in the third Hrabanus Maurus turns first to basic education (the "liberal arts") and then to theological instruction. As many similar books, this work borrowed heavily from the *Institutions* of Cassiodorus and from Augustine's *On Christian Doctrine.* Its impact was such that Hrabanus Maurus was given the title of *Praeceptor Germaniae* or "teacher of Germany"—a title that much later would be given also to Melanchthon.

The Carolingian renaissance was brief, for soon the Frankish kingdom was divided among various heirs, while the increasing threats and invasions by the Normans brought chaos to the land. During the reign of Charles the Bald (840–77), there was a brief period of peace and prosperity, allowing the king to implement part of Charlemagne's program of education. But chaos soon returned, and the Middle Ages were once again submerged in darkness.

However, even during that time, a number of monastic and cathedral schools continued functioning, and it was they who preserved the knowledge of antiquity—both Christian and Greco-Roman—until better conditions would once more allow for more original study, research, and teaching.

In summary, the first Germanic invasions were followed by a period of chaos and obscurantism during which monastic and cathedral schools played a crucial role in the preservation and dissemination of knowledge. Although under Charlemagne and some of his successors there were some periods of relative peace and order, in general chaos and ignorance seemed to reign until the end of the eleventh century. During all that time, even though many pastors were trained in cathedral and monastic schools, most priests did not have the advantages of such an education, and there was no concerted program to make it available to them. Furthermore, most of the clerics who did study employed their knowledge in positions of administration or teaching—which is seen to this day in that many of those employed in administration are called "clerks," and their work is "clerical."

6

The Beginnings of Scholasticism

For a number of reasons, several of them having to do with contacts with the Muslim world, in the twelfth century Western Europe enjoyed a renewal that had both economic and intellectual dimensions. Despite the unjustifiable cruelty and bloodshed and the resulting hostility, the Crusades fostered contact and trade between Western Christendom and the Muslim world. That commercial expansion in turn brought about the growth of cities and the rebirth of the monetary economy—which during the darker period had been replaced by a barter system. As part of this renewal there was also an awakening of letters and knowledge. Within that awakening, four persons are particularly worthy of note, for their writings were the foundation of the great theological enterprise that flourished beginning in the thirteenth century, which is usually called "scholasticism." These four authors were Anselm, Abelard, Hugh of Saint Victor, and Peter Lombard.

Anselm, an Italian by birth, was prior of the monastery of Bec in Normandy—one of the great monasteries that the Normans had founded after their conversion—and then became archbishop of Canterbury. He is particularly known today for his famous "ontological argument" to prove the existence of God and also for his treatise *Why Did God Become Human?* where he proposes the view that the work of Jesus is a payment for sin. But equally important is the manner in which Anselm understood the theological enterprise, for this would be the perspective driving the best scholastic theologians. The aim of Anselm's theology was not to systematize Christian truths nor to discover the secrets of

37

God nor even to direct other believers but rather to express and to experience his own love of God and God's truth. Thus, at the beginning of his *Proslogion* he says:

> I am not trying, O Lord, to penetrate thy loftiness, for I cannot begin to match my understanding with it, but I desire in some measure to understand thy truth, which my heart believes and loves. For I do not seek to understand in order to believe, but I believe in order to understand. For this too I believe, that "unless I believe, I shall not understand."[1]

This may be seen in his two works dealing with the existence of God—the *Monologion* and the *Proslogion*—as well as in his treatise on the reason for the incarnation—*Why Did God Become Human?* Anselm had no doubt about the existence of God—furthermore, his entire *Proslogion* is framed as a prayer to God. Nor did he doubt that Jesus died for his sins. His purpose was simply to better understand what he already believed, and he did this because of his love for God and the gospel.

The perspective of Peter Abelard—normally known simply as Abelard—was quite different. His brief autobiography, *Historia calamitatum*—a history of calamities—shows him to be an exceptionally intelligent person but also one having an almost unnatural need to prove his own intelligence. The result was that Abelard broke with all his teachers one after the other. When he finally was able to begin teaching in the cathedral of Paris, his love affair with Heloise brought further tragedy to his life. His most remarkable work is the book *Sic et non—Yes and no*—where he poses one hundred fifty-eight theological questions on which authorities—that is, scriptures and the "Fathers" of the church—seem to be mutually contradictory. Abelard's purpose was not to belittle the authority of these ancient writings, but rather to show off his wide range of knowledge and to demonstrate that things are not as simple as one might imagine. But his work was not well received, and this and his other writings simply gained him more enemies—among them the influential Saint Bernard of Clairvaux. However, as we shall see, *Sic et non* set the pattern for the scholastic method as a whole.

Hugh of Saint Victor was the most famous theologian of the "school of Saint Victor." The Abbey of Saint Victor was founded about the year 1110 in the outskirts of Paris, on the western bank of the Seine. It followed the rule of the Canons of Saint Augustine. Soon a series of distinguished thinkers brought international fame to the school in that abbey—thinkers such as William of Champeaux (1068–121) and Richard of Saint Victor (who died in 1173).

Hugh joined Saint Victor in 1015 when he was some thirty years old, and eighteen years later was put in charge of the abbey's program of studies and teaching. He was convinced that all knowledge comes from God, and that therefore all knowledge leads to God. Following the Augustinian tradition that held sway in the first centuries of the Middle Ages, Hugh saw the entire creation as a sign or symbol pointing toward its Creator. In discussing the totality of human knowledge, he placed philosophy above the liberal arts, and theology above philosophy. Philosophy includes all knowledge that reason may attain—what he calls things "according to reason"—while theological knowledge comes from revelation and is therefore "above reason"—*supra rationem*. But their being above reason does not mean that they contradict it. This view of the difference and the hierarchical relationship between philosophy and theology shaped the entire curriculum of the nascent universities. And his distinction between truths of reason and those that are above reason was the foundation of the theological work of thinkers such as Saint Thomas Aquinas and other great scholastic theologians.

The importance of Hugh's work lies in the manner in which, in combining his own mystical and contemplative tendencies with the use of reason—or "dialectics," as rational enquiry was then called—he undid much of the bad opinion that many had of the use of reason in theology. Much of this bad opinion was due to Abelard's work. Hugh, while rejecting the "errors" of Abelard, repeatedly quoted him with respect and admiration. This in turn opened the way for Abelard's *Sic et non* to shape the scholastic method.

Also, since it relates to the subject at hand, it may be worthwhile to quote Hugh's opinion on study and its purpose:

> Therefore I beg you, reader, not to rejoice too much for having read much, if you have not understood much. Nor should you rejoice at having understood much, if you are not able to retain much. Because if you have not done this, reading or understanding does you little good.[2]

However, the most influential among all the forerunners of scholasticism was Peter Lombard, so called because he came from Lombardy. He was first a teacher in the cathedral school of Paris and then bishop of that city. His main work, *Four Books of Sentences*, was an entire systematic theology, which set the traditional outline of similar works for centuries to come: God and the Trinity (book i), creation and sin (book ii), the incarnation and the ethical life (book iii), and sacraments and eschatology (book iv).

Like Anselm, Peter Lombard wrote within the context of a profound devotion. He thus declares that "the truth of the one who gave truth to us [God] causes great pleasure; but the immensity of the task causes great fear. The desire to move forward inspires us; but the weakness of failure discourages us. But the zeal for the house of the Lord overcomes such weakness."[3]

On the other hand, Peter is also aware of the danger of idle curiosity and above all of the danger of those who simply seek to say something new—an attitude that was beginning to appear in the schools and that many attributed to Abelard. In strong words, Peter Lombard criticizes those:

> ...who seek to mold the words of wisdom after their own dreams. They do not subject their will to reason, nor devote themselves to the study of doctrine. They seek a reason that does not lead them to truth, but to pleasure. They do not wish to learn the truth, but turn away from it to fables. They are more concerned with pleasure than with what is to be taught, and with adapting doctrine to their own desire. Their words sound pious, but lack conscience. Their lying words are in truth impious. For they corrupt the sanctity of faith by teaching false doctrine and promoting in others an itching of the ears.[4]

In contrast to this, Peter Lombard declares that his purpose is to exalt the light, placing it on the candlestick, and therefore "with much toil and sweat," but with the help of God, he has compiled his four books. The word *compile* is a sign of what Peter attempts to do. He is not trying to write a vast summa, nor to show his own ability for innovation, but rather to compile "the sentences of the Fathers in a single volume," which should serve the reader in such a way "that it will no longer be necessary to open many books, so that one may find what one seeks without excessive toil."[5] Finally, Peter Lombard declares himself ready to listen to "correctors," but at the same time hopes that his book will result in more "discoverers" than "correctors."

This last wish was not immediately fulfilled. Since Peter Lombard's "compilation" went far beyond the mere collecting of quotations from the Bible and from ancient Christian writings, and included a good number of commentaries of his own, it was severely criticized and attacked. Some even declared it heretical. Finally, in 1215—45 years after the death of Peter Lombard—the Fourth Lateran Council vindicated him, not only declaring him orthodox but also adopting his views on several points—among them, the list of the seven sacraments, which the council took from the *Sentences*. The work of this council was simply an affirmation of a vast number of policies, doctrines, and decrees prepared by Innocent III, the most powerful pope in all history, and therefore it can be said that it was Innocent who commended the work of Peter Lombard. From that time on, the *Sentences* of Peter Lombard became the main textbook for theological studies. As we shall see, the theological curriculum of the University of Paris—and soon also of others such as Oxford and Salamanca—stipulated that any candidate for a master's degree should spend some time as a "bachelor of the sentences," commenting on the *Sentences* of Peter Lombard.

In summary, toward the end of the eleventh century and throughout the twelfth there was an economic and intellectual awakening in Western Europe. The growing monetary economy was overcoming the barter economy, which had been dominant for centuries. This was both a consequence of and a cause for a network of communication and trade that became ever wider. This brought with itself the growth of cities, and therefore also of cathedral schools. Slowly but inevitably, cathedral schools would eventually overcome those in monasteries, which were most frequently to be found in rural areas. Soon, as we shall see, this concentration of studies in the cities would lead to the founding of the first universities.

As part of this awakening of the late eleventh century and of the twelfth, there were a number of thinkers who would be forerunners of the scholasticism of the thirteenth. Among them one must pay particular attention to Anselm, Hugh Saint Victor, Abelard, and Peter Lombard. Although these were very different among themselves, they all contributed in one way or another to the awakening of theology and of studies in general that would take place in the thirteenth century.

Although all of these were teachers in one way or another, and even though many of their disciples were pastors, their main purpose was not to prepare candidates for pastoral ministry but rather to inquire about truth itself—as Anselm would say, of God's "truth which my heart believes and loves." This too would be characteristic of the best work of the universities where scholasticism flourished, for the purpose of universities was not so much ministerial education as it was philosophical and contemplative inquiry.

7

The Universities and Scholasticism

The intellectual awakening of the twelfth century led to the creation of conglomerations of students and professors that would eventually be called "universities." These were the heirs that continued the traditions created by monastic and cathedral schools, as may be clearly seen in the history of the University of Paris, the most famous of the early universities—particularly in the field of theology. One of many factors that had earlier attracted students to the abbey of Saint Victor was the manner in which that school joined the use of reason with mystical contemplation—a joining that would be the ideal, not often achieved, of the theological faculties in the University of Paris as well as others. For that reason, many came to Saint Victor seeking theological learning, not so much to serve as ministers or pastors but rather for their own spiritual and intellectual development.

The history itself, first of the Abbey of Saint Victor and then of the University of Paris, is a sign of the dual origin of universities, born both out of monastic schools and out of cathedral schools. William of Champeaux had taught in the cathedral school of Notre Dame in Paris. There he clashed with Abelard, who was prone to show his exceptional intellect by belittling his professors. Defeated, or at least discouraged, William abandoned the cathedral school and settled in Saint Victor, whose school became a rival of the one at the cathedral. Given the fame of that school, as well as of other teachers, in a few generations there were more students on the western bank of the Seine, in and around Saint Victor than in the cathedral school of Notre Dame, even though the latter was still growing. On the western side of the river, around the year 1160, the various teachers began

43

organizing as a guild whose main purpose was to insure the quality of their studies by certifying them with a measure of uniformity. Since the word *universitas* was then what today we call a guild or a union, that consortium of teachers and students came to be known as the "university." Traditionally it was the chancellor of the cathedral school of Notre Dame who had the authority to certify studies and to grant licenses for teaching, and therefore there soon were serious conflicts between the cathedral school and the new guild or "university" that was being formed. Finally, in 1211 Pope Innocent III granted a charter for the University of Paris, and soon the conflicts began to abate so that eventually the university and the ancient cathedral school were joined in one.

Several other universities would follow the example of Paris. The university in Bologna specialized in law and that in Salerno in medicine. But those in Paris, Oxford, and Salamanca, among many others, were particularly noted for their philosophical and theological studies.

One of the main methods of teaching in medieval universities was the *lectio*—or lecture—in which the professor commented on a text. This was to be done following the order of the book being commented on, sometimes even word by word. Apparently, at the very beginning the most common lectures were commentaries on books of the Bible. But soon it became customary to comment also on the four books of *Sentences* of Peter Lombard. It was expected that each student would bring to class a copy of the text being commented. But the high cost of books led many to borrow or even rent those pages of the book that were about to be commented on, or to make their own copies. In any case, it was customary to have an advanced student read aloud the text to be discussed. The professor's commentary consisted of a series of questions put to the text and to which the professor was to respond following the scholastic method that will be described in a moment, which was perfected in the *disputationes*.

As to the manner in which lectures were to be conducted, there was some debate—and there still is—as may be seen in the following excerpt from the charter of the University of Paris:

> Two methods of lecturing...have been tried, the former masters of philosophy uttering their words rapidly so that the mind of the hearer can take them in but the hand cannot keep up with them, the latter speaking slowly until their listeners can catch up with them with the pen; having compared these by diligent examination, the former method is found the better. Wherefore, the consensus of opinion warns us that we imitate it in our lectures. We, therefore, all and each, ... shall observe the former method of lecturing to the best of our ability, so speaking forsooth as if no one was taking notes from them... Moreover, transgressors of this statute... we now

deprive henceforth for a year from lecturing, honors, offices and other advantages of our faculty.

And, to show that this was an issue, not only among faculty but also among students, the statute goes on to establish penalties for "listeners who oppose the execution of this our statute by clamor, hissing noise, or throwing stones by themselves or by their servants and accomplices."[1]

Another commonly used method was the debate—*disputatio*—which appeared first in the faculty of theology in Paris and quickly expanded to other disciplines as well as to other universities. There were two sorts of *disputatio*: the *disputatio ordinaria* and the *disputatio de quodlibet*. The *disputatio ordinaria* took place with relative frequency—often weekly—and was less demanding academically than the *de quodlibet*. Normally, the *disputatio ordinaria*, since it took place regularly, followed a set theme or text, which was then discussed and clarified with each successive *disputatio*.

In this exercise, the professor posed a thesis or question to be discussed. An advanced student or a group of them—the *opponents*—proposed a series of arguments that would seem mutually contradictory, for some would lend support to a response and some to the opposite view. Usually such arguments consisted in quotes from authoritative texts—above all the Bible, the "Fathers" of the church, and sometimes the classical philosophers—or were based on widely acknowledged logical principles. It was then the task of another advanced student—the *respondent*—to offer a response based on the arguments adduced for one side and also to explain why the apparently opposing arguments did not contradict the answer that the student gave. Finally the professor, in another session, would offer a more careful and detailed response, which was called his *determinatio*.

The *disputatio de quodlibet* was much less formal in its structure but much more difficult and therefore of greater importance in university life. For this reason it was celebrated only once or twice a year—in Advent and Lent—and always under the direction of a "regent professor"—that is, a doctor. Its very name—roughly meaning "disputation on whatever you please"—indicates that there was much more freedom in the selection of the subject. In contrast to the *disputatio ordinaria*, which took place in the classroom and only in the presence of students, the *disputatio de quodlibet* was open to the public. In this event students as well as professors and even the public at large could pose questions and offer arguments and objections. Since there were frequent rivalries among professors, it was not rare for a teacher to take this opportunity to ridicule his rivals. And since the subject was much more flexible, the professor could not have prepared his answers beforehand. Once the arguments for and against the response were posed, the teacher had a few days to prepare his *determinatio*, in which he had to respond to all the arguments and objections against his answers.

This process of posing a thesis or question, then offering arguments and authorities that apparently contradict one another, giving an answer, and finally showing why the authorities that appear to take another position do not contradict what the professor has determined, is the core of the scholastic method. In this one can clearly see the influence of Abelard's *Sic et non*, with its quotations from apparently contradictory authorities. But one can also see the interest of Hugh of Saint Victor and Peter Lombard, that the conflict among such apparently contradictory authorities be resolved in such a way that their value is not questioned nor diminished.

The university curriculum began with three or four years devoted to the study of the seven liberal arts—that is, the *trivium* and the *quadrivium*. This was followed by a rigorous series of public and oral examinations on these various arts. After passing these exams, the student was a "bachelor." Although practice varied from university to university, those who would then continue studying theology were now called "biblical bachelors," and for two years would give lectures on the Bible. Originally, the first year was devoted to an exegesis of a single book in the Old Testament, and the second to one in the New, but slowly this custom was abandoned so that there were biblical bachelors who lectured on several books. Once this requirement was completed to the satisfaction of the faculty, the biblical bachelor became a "sententiary bachelor," whose main academic exercise consisted of commenting in detail on the *Four Books of Sentences* of Peter Lombard. Normally, these commentaries followed the scholastic method of the *quaestiones disputatae*, with the arguments for and against an answer, the *determinatio* by the bachelor, and his response to the apparently contradictory authorities. In these exercises, the future professor could not use the works of other teachers or commentators but rather had to produce his own material on the basis not only of the *Sentences* themselves but also of the Bible, the "Fathers," classical philosophers, and logic. It was thus expected that, through a process lasting some two years, the sententiary bachelor would develop his own thought.

After satisfactorily completing at least two years of commenting on the *Sentences*, the student became a "formed bachelor." As such, he could teach and preach at the university, always under the supervision of a licensed teacher. This period would normally take several years—eventually set at a minimum of five years. During this time the formed bachelor also had to participate as "respondent" in at least one *quaestio disputata de quodlibet*. Since in this exercise the prospective professor, serving as "respondent," had to deal with any questions posed by his professors as well as by other students and even by the public at large, what was being measured was, beyond the student's knowledge, his ability to respond with solid biblical and theological foundations to any question that might be posed. Finally, after that long process and a careful examination of his moral life and his dedication to study, the formed bachelor became a "master" or "doctor," which now allowed him to preside independently over *quaestiones disputatae*— both the more common or ordinary ones and those *de quodlibet*—as well as to lecture and to preach at the university. Given the length of this process, normally those who became doctors attained this degree well after forty years of age.

The professors were clergymen and most of the students also were ordained, since a common way to cover the cost of studies was to receive the benefits of an ecclesiastical position to which the student was named but where another performed the pastoral duties. As was to be expected, the number of actual pastors who had university studies was minimal. Therefore, although today the universities, their great teachers, and their literary and theological production occupy the attention of historians, the truth is that still the monastic, diocesan, and parochial schools continued being the place where the vast majority of pastors were formed. The more complicated and prolonged university studies became, the greater was the number of clergymen who did not have them.

This gave rise to a situation parallel to what has happened in more recent times: university studies became increasingly specialized but at the same time increasingly distant from parochial life as well as from the interests of those who practiced pastoral ministry. This does not mean that the professors and students at universities were not deeply religious. On the contrary, most of them seem to have devoted themselves to theological studies on the basis of a firm commitment to the Christian faith and a profound conviction that their studies would help them grow in faith. This may be seen in two incidents or stories told about the two greatest teachers of the University of Paris in the thirteenth century, Bonaventure and Thomas Aquinas. Of Bonaventure, usually called the "Seraphic Doctor," it is said that when Thomas, the "Angelic Doctor," asked him to show him the library from which his ample knowledge was derived, Bonaventure answered by showing him a crucifix. Although there is every probability that this never took place, it certainly reflects the attitude of Bonaventure as is known to us through his writings. Thomas, after writing the voluminous works that guaranteed his fame to this day, had a mystical experience that would lead him to declare that, when compared to what he had seen, all that he had written was like straw. After that time he wrote very little.

But it is also important to point out that both Bonaventure and Thomas Aquinas brought to the university a renewed spirituality thanks to the impact of the mendicant orders—the Franciscans in the case of Bonaventure and the Dominicans in that of Saint Thomas. It is necessary therefore to take a moment to say a brief word about the origins of those orders and their impact on the manner in which people understood the ordained ministry.

Both orders were born in the thirteenth century, and their enormous success and attraction were due to the manner in which they were a creative and relevant response to the new conditions of that century. Their emphasis on poverty—particularly strong in Saint Francis but also present in Saint Dominic—may be seen as a reaction to the growing impersonality of the monetary economy in contrast with the earlier barter economy. The success of both orders was also due to the manner in which they were an answer to the demographic challenges of the time. Due to the rapid growth of cities, the older parochial system was unable to respond to the spiritual needs of all believers. Therefore, the mendicant orders, with their greater geographic flexibility, helped the church to provide ministerial services to the masses that were gathered in the cities. But their success was due above all to the manner in which they combined devotion with action and voluntary poverty with service to the poor. Their arrival at the universities counteracted the tendencies of those institutions to distance themselves from the church. The Dominicans had been interested in studies from the very beginning, for Saint Dominic founded his order to counteract the heresies that abounded in southern France, and the refutation of such heresies required solid intellectual instruments. Therefore, Dominican houses were also centers of biblical and theological studies. The most famous of these convents was the one in Paris, founded in 1217, and whose main teacher was Roland of Cremona. When, amidst its disputes with the chancellor of the cathedral school, the university was temporarily dissolved, many of its students went to the Dominican house to continue their studies, with the result that when the university was reorganized, Roland of Cremona became one of its professors—and therefore the first Dominican teacher at the university. When professor Jean de Saint Giles joined the Dominicans, that order had two professors in the university guild. Something similar took place in Oxford, when professor Robert Bacon became a Dominican in 1227. Soon the Dominicans had an important place in all theological faculties. Among them the most famous and influential was Saint Thomas Aquinas, to whom we shall return.

The history of Franciscan presence in the universities—particularly in the University of Paris—was somewhat different. Saint Francis had not shown any great interest in academic studies, either for himself or for his followers, and therefore at the beginning those followers did not seek a place in the universities. But in 1236 the university professor Alexander of Hales became a Franciscan, and this was the first entry of the Order of Friars Minor into the University of Paris. Since then, in a process parallel to that of the Dominicans, the Franciscan presence in the university grew both in numbers and in prestige. The most famous among Franciscan teacher in the thirteenth century was Saint Bonaventure, to whom we shall also return.

The presence of mendicants—Franciscans as well as Dominicans—among the university professors was not well received by many of their colleagues. Until that time, university teaching had been in the hands of diocesan clergy who had no vows of poverty, and many of these professors resented the emphasis of the mendicants on poverty, since it seemed to be an attack on their own lifestyle. The controversy broke out in the middle of the thirteenth century, when the procurator of the university, William of Saint Amour, after failing in his attempts to expel the Franciscans, wrote two works in which he claimed that the position of the mendicants regarding "evangelical poverty" was heretical. The virulence of his attack may be seen in the very titles of his two works: *On the Antichrist* (1254) and *On the Dangers of the Present Times* (1256). After Pope Alexander IV condemned these works and King Louis IX of France (Saint Louis) ordered that their author be exiled, another professor, Gerard D'Abbeville, took the lead in the struggle against the mendicants.

The importance of this conflict for the matter at hand is not so much in the issue of poverty itself as in what it implied for the lifestyle of students and professors, as well as for their methods of study. For several generations, as the importance of monastic schools waned and that of cathedral schools waxed, eventually leading to the founding of universities, the emphasis on community living as the proper context for study had been declining. In monastic schools, belonging to the community was not a matter of convenience but rather a requirement and the necessary context for studies themselves. In cathedral schools, and later in the universities, although the latter were guilds and even though frequently students shared resources and living quarters, this was only done as a means to facilitate their studies, no longer as part of the very understanding of such studies and their purpose. In contrast, both Dominicans and Franciscans saw the communities to which they belonged as the point of departure, the context and the goal of their studies and of their entire lives. For them, the principle of "evangelical poverty," in which all share all available resources, was important not only as an ascetic practice or as a "counsel of perfection" but also as a necessary practice for life in close community. Therefore, even though the Franciscans soon abandoned their founder's ideal of absolute poverty, both they and the Dominicans insisted on individual poverty, since all they had belonged to the community and not to the individual.

In contrast to such attitudes, the "secular" teachers—that is, those who did not belong to monastic communities, since they were all clergymen, and no teacher was "secular" in today's meaning of the word—underscored individual achievement. They covered their expenses mostly with the fees they charged their

49

students. It is easy to imagine the rivalry and competition resulting from this situation, which would be acrimoniously expressed and strengthened in exercises such as the *quaestiones disputatae*—particularly those *de quodlibet*. Therefore, the debate between "seculars" and "religious" not only was about poverty but had far-reaching consequences for the manner in which the educational process was understood and how it related to the actual lives of students and professors.

Furthermore, as is generally known, the thirteenth century, particularly in the University of Paris, but soon throughout Christendom, witnessed long debates resulting from the reintroduction into Western Europe of the works of Aristotle, as well as those of his commentator Averroes and other Arab and Jewish philosophers. The contrasting manners in which this impacted educational philosophy as well as theology may be seen by comparing the writings of Bonaventure on the teacher and his function with those of Thomas Aquinas.

On this subject, Bonaventure produced three treatises that are similar and mutually complementary: *Reductio artium ad theologiam*—*The reduction of the sciences to theology, Christus, unus omnium magister*—*Christ, the only teacher of all*, and *De excellentia magisterii Christi*—*On the excellence of Christ's teaching*. In them, Bonaventure simply wishes to reaffirm what had been said earlier by Saint Augustine, that all true knowledge comes from Christ and that the function of the human teacher is not to teach but rather to point to the inner knowledge that Christ gives. In the *Reduction* he makes an inventory and summary of all the sciences and arts that were studied at the time in order to show that in all of them knowledge is an illumination coming from Christ. The second work mentioned above follows the general guidelines of Saint Augustine's *De magistro*, although without spending as much time as Augustine did on philosophical matters having to do with how words signify. In the third, he leaves aside the function of any human teacher in order to claim that "regarding all that has to be believed, and against the untruth of error, Christ truly teaches in the most delightful way."[2]

On his part, Thomas Aquinas discussed the subject in his *quastiones disputatae* (number xi), as well as in *De magistro* and in his *Summa Theologica*.[3] In all these writings Thomas assigns the teacher a much more active function than either Augustine or Bonaventure did. According to him, the teacher leads the disciple from what is known to the unknown but at the same time makes him see the connections among various principles and conclusions. This may be seen in his answer to a question on whether a human being can teach at all:

Now the master leads the disciple from things known to knowledge of the unknown, in a twofold manner. Firstly, by proposing to him certain helps or means of instruction, which his intellect can use for the acquisition of science: for instance,

50

he may put before him certain less universal propositions, of which nevertheless the disciple is able to judge from previous knowledge: or he may propose to him some sensible examples, either by way of likeness or of opposition, or something of the sort, from which the intellect of the learner is led to the knowledge of truth previously unknown. Secondly, by strengthening the intellect of the learner; not, indeed, by some active power as of a higher nature,...but inasmuch as he proposes to the disciple the order of principles to conclusions, by reason of his not having sufficient collating power to be able to draw the conclusions from the principles.[4]

The difference between Augustine and Bonaventure on the one hand and Saint Thomas on the other is due to the reintroduction of Aristotle and to Thomas's interest in bringing together the long Platonic and Augustinian tradition with the Aristotelian theory of knowledge. Therefore, although Thomas still refers to knowledge as "illumination," this does not mean the same as it did for Augustine and Bonaventure. For the latter two, "illumination" comes from on high, from the word of God. What Saint Thomas understands by "illumination," rather than a gift from on high, is a process through which the mind discovers the essence of a number of interrelated sensations—what Thomas knows as an "image" or a "phantom." That image—for instance, that of a horse—comes to us through the senses and is necessary for knowledge. But knowledge is not absolutely true unless it is knowledge of essences. True knowledge is achieved when, through the process that Thomas calls "illumination," the mind abstracts from the image of a horse the very idea of "horse." It is this manner of understanding knowledge that gives the teacher a function that is more active and necessary than it was in the ancient Platonic and Augustinian tradition, for knowledge is in the disciple only potentially, and the function of the teacher is to actualize it.

One may then say that the reintroduction of the philosophy of Aristotle and the manner in which Thomas Aquinas adapted that philosophy to theology and to Christian teaching led to a drastic revolution in the manner in which both teaching and knowledge itself were understood. That revolution was such that without it, it is impossible to conceive modern science, which is based precisely on the observation of sensory data—and on experimentation, which is controlled observation—in order then to abstract from them general conclusions that go beyond particular cases.

Returning to the subject of ministerial education, it is clear that much of the theology that was studied, discussed, and produced in the universities had no great relevance for ministerial practice. The great *Summa Theologica* of Saint Thomas, as well as the *Commentaries on the Sentences* of the most famous theologians, is a voluminous work that could be found only in a few select libraries, particularly those in the larger universities. And even if it had been available to the common pastor, the subjects that were discussed in it were so abstract and detailed that it would have been of little use for their pastoral labors.

This does not mean, however, that the work of those theologians was lacking in value. As we have already seen, it is difficult to envision the development of Western science without Thomas Aquinas. Thus, it would be wrong to judge that work only in terms of its applicability to the daily life of the church. Furthermore, such a judgment would be based on a pragmatic attitude that judges the value of knowledge only in terms of its usefulness. But the vision of all great medieval teachers—a vision inspired by Augustine and others—was of a theology born not so much from the needs of those who read the theologian's work as from the love of the theologian for God and God's truth. According to this vision, theology is close to contemplation, and it is an expression of the love of God with all the mind.

Furthermore, despite their abstractions, several of those scholastic theologians were deeply concerned for the formation and instruction of pastors and missionaries. Thus, for instance, it is quite possible that the *Summa Contra Gentiles* of Thomas Aquinas—much briefer than the *Summa Theologica*, but still fairly voluminous—was conceived, at least in part, as a handbook for those undertaking missionary work among Muslims or facing them in debates. And Bonaventure's *Breviloquium*, one of the most copied and read writings during the thirteenth and fourteenth centuries, was written, according to Bonaventure himself, because:

> ...upon the request of my associates that from my poor knowledge I say something briefly in a *summa* about the truth of theology, I have consented to set down a kind of compendium in which I do not deal with all things summarily, but treat briefly of certain things that it is more important to know.[5]

All of this shows that, in spite of the apparent coldness and rigidity of scholastic writings, among the great teachers of early scholasticism the spirit still prevailed of Saint Francis and Saint Dominic, for whom the church and community life were an essential part of theology, as well as the spirit of Anselm, for whom study was an act of devotion.

In summary, the thirteenth century saw a great surge in theological studies that has no parallel in the entire history of Christianity. It has been well said that Saint Thomas's *Summa Theologica* is like a great Gothic cathedral, where the entire universe is included and where diverse elements counterbalance one another in such a way that the entire building rises to unexpected heights. And we must not forget that this famous work is only the best-known and most influential among dozens of summae and other writings of incredibly erudite authors.

As in the case of Anselm, the great scholastic teachers of the thirteenth century were people of profound piety for whom their studies and discussions were simply one more way of showing their love for God with all their mind. This was particularly true of the Franciscans and Dominicans, who soon became an important presence in the schools of theology of universities such as Paris, Oxford, and Salamanca. Thanks to the manner in which these orders underscored the importance of community life, the best teachers of the thirteenth century were able to set limits to the individualistic rivalry that would eventually become a mark of university life—and which the debates involved in the scholastic method, even unwittingly, nourished.

But this theological awakening did not result in better preparation for the majority of the clergy—particularly for pastors in poor or rural parishes. Very few of them ever visited a university, and the cost of books was such that they were practically out of reach even for those among the clergy who were able to read with some fluency—and these were relatively few.

8
The Last Centuries of the Middle Ages

Although historians—particularly those interested in the history of thought and of theology—have paid much attention to the universities and their professors, the fact is that the proportion of clergymen who had university studies was minimal. In spite of the growth of cities, still most of the flock lived in rural areas, where the parish priest was not expected to know much. Due to the lack of surviving documents—and to the parallel lack of studies on those that have survived—it is very difficult to determine the educational level of parish priests in villages and small towns, as well as of those who served in urban parishes of lesser importance. There are many documents decreeing that every parish should have a school for the children of the area. But the very fact that those orders had to be repeated again and again is an indication that they were not always obeyed. Although in the larger and richer parishes it was frequent to have a teacher devoted to the parochial school, most frequently in small parishes it was the priest who also served as teacher. At any rate, what was taught in those schools was so elemental that in many cases it was not even necessary for the teacher to know how to read. Frequently those studies were limited to learning by heart the Lord's Prayer, the Creed, the Ten Commandments, and some of the more common prayers. Thus, one frequently finds references to priests who had no more knowledge than what they had learned by heart in order to celebrate the mass and other rites.

Furthermore, by then there was a fairly uniform hierarchy of clerical orders—which had long varied from place to place both in the number of orders and in the names given to them. Commonly, these orders were divided between the "minor" and the "major." The four minor orders were doorkeeper, reader, exorcist, and acolyte; and the three major orders were deacon, presbyter, and bishop. The responsibilities of the doorkeeper only had to do with opening and closing the church, inviting those to Communion who were "worthy," and making sure that the "unworthy" did not partake of it. The reader's main responsibility was to read the biblical text on which preaching was to be based—if there was preaching, for many cases there was no sermon—and teaching the catechism, which was no longer a preparation for baptism, as in the ancient church, but actually teaching the rudiments of the faith to children who had been baptized as infants. In the Western church, the anointing that had earlier been part of the baptismal rites now was separated from it and became a different sacrament, confirmation. This was now usually administered to children who had reached the age of responsibility—normally, seven years of age—and had received some basic instruction, which now was called "catechism." Since the catechism was learned and taught by rote, all the education that the reader needed—and frequently did not have—was to know how to read.[1] The exorcist—an order that was later eliminated—was in charge of praying for the sick and casting out demons. And, last among the minor orders, the acolyte helped the priest in the service of the mass.

In theory, the "major orders"—deacon, presbyter, and bishop—required a certain degree of knowledge. But there was not an established plan of studies, nor any definition of what it was necessary to know in order to receive such orders or to occupy the positions connected with them. Even during the thirteenth and fourteenth centuries, when the universities were flourishing, there were abundant cases of illiterate priests and even bishops. And it was not uncommon to have a child consecrated as a bishop thanks to the advocacy and the money of his family.

This leads us to consider another element that impinged on ministerial studies, namely corruption. Corruption had become widespread much earlier, in part as a result of the Germanic invasions and the ensuing chaos, in part as a consequence of the feudal system that those invasions brought about, and in part because the church was becoming ever richer and more powerful and therefore ecclesiastical positions became more desirable.

Feudalism was based on a system of "benefices," which normally consisted of lands that a feudal lord would grant to a vassal as a reward for a service rendered or promised. Although at first such benefices were limited to the duration of the lives of both the grantor and the grantee, they progressively became hereditary, and it was this division of lands—and therefore of wealth and authority—that gave rise to feudalism.

Within the church there soon was a similar system. Parishes, dioceses, and other ecclesiastical positions became "benefices," which, even though not hereditary like secular fiefdoms, remained even after feudalism began to decline and were part of the structure of ecclesiastical life throughout the Middle Ages. Thus, a priest receiving a benefice lived from the rents that the benefice itself produced—tithes, offerings, and the yield of the lands belonging to the parish. Since the younger sons of rich families could not inherit the property of their parents, one of the ways in which the latter made provision for them was directing them to an ecclesiastical career and making sure that they had a benefice. Therefore, although in theory the benefices were only a system of providing sustenance for pastors and other servants of the church, in truth they were normally granted thanks to the patronage of an influential person—the family and friends of the beneficiary, the bishop, a secular patron, and so forth. Frequently, the studies and ability of the candidate to occupy the position and fulfill its functions were of little or no concern. In other words, thanks to the benefice that was attached to pastoral functions, the determining factor deciding who would occupy such positions was similar to the ancient relations between a patron and his client.[2] What this implied for ministerial training is evident: that training consisted mostly of the necessary steps to obtain the patronage of a nobleman or a prelate and that not much was required in terms of academic preparation or even of pastoral abilities.

This does not mean that people were not concerned over such state of affairs. On the contrary, the last centuries of the Middle Ages abounded in decrees, steps, and programs whose purpose was to improve the training of the clergy. In order to show this, a glance at what was taking place in the Iberian Peninsula suffices, for this was typical of the entire continent.[3] In 1228, a council gathered in Valladolid ordered that all priests should be given three years in order to learn Latin. During those three years, their stipends would be withheld. And, if at the end of that period they had not learned enough Latin, they were to be deposed. In 1303 another council gathered in León decreed that, besides being legitimate children, candidates to major orders must be able to read and chant, besides knowing by heart the canon of the mass and the words and gestures proper to the main rites of the church. The same was ordered in Oporto in 1494 and in several other regional councils, as well as in the decrees of several governments and prelates.

But such decrees and measures did not remedy the situation. In order not to be too demanding, it soon became common not to apply such requirements to children under ten years of age nor to the "elderly" who were more than thirty-five, as may be seen in the decisions of the bishop of Avila Alonso Ulloa y de Fonseca in the middle of the fifteenth century (1445–54). (It is necessary to point out that the very fact that children under ten years of age could be enjoying ecclesiastical benefices is a further indication of the reigning corruption. And, to make things worse, it was not only priests who could be appointed at such an early age but even bishops and abbots). In 1293, the main teacher in the cathedral school of Valencia was illiterate. Somewhat later, the prelates in Avila complained that even in the cathedral itself there were clergymen who hardly knew how to read. In 1325 another council in Segovia ordered that in the cathedral schools of archdioceses theology be taught, while all that was required in schools in the other dioceses was limited to grammar, logic, and rhetoric—that is, the ancient *trivium*, although now instead of astronomy, which required some mathematical knowledge, logic was to be studied.

In spite of the sad state of letters among most of the secular clergy, there were also many others who sought to study further. Many of the teachers in cathedral schools had studied in universities, and the same is true of some prelates. Among them, one may mention by way of example Alonso Fernández de Madrigal, who studied in the University of Salamanca and succeeded Fonseca as bishop of Avila in 1454. Known as *el Tostado*—the Toasted—apparently because of his dark skin,[4] Fernández de Madrigal wrote erudite commentaries on several books of the Bible, as well as on some of the writings of Augustine and Jerome. Among his works there is a treatise *On the Best Policy* in which he proposes democracy as the best form of government. In several other dioceses besides Avila were other bishops who were good students of theology. Just to give one more example, one must not forget that Peter Lombard—the author of the *Sentences*—was bishop of Paris from 1159 to 1160 and that the same diocese had as its bishops other famous theologians such as William of Auvergne (1249) and Étienne Tempier (1250–68).

But even these bishops were able to do little regarding the basic knowledge of a good number of the clergy under their supervision. Many of these clergymen had received benefices thanks to the support of powerful patrons, and the bishops had little power to force them to study. And, if such was the case of bishops who were concerned over the training and pastoral abilities of the clergy, much worse must have been the case among others whose bishops were less conscientious, for they themselves owed their positions to patronage.

The system of benefices became increasingly corrupt, and this in turn resulted in paying less attention to the training of clergy to serve in parishes and also led to an even greater distance between the university chair and parish life. Normally, those who served a parish or occupied another ecclesiastical charge as a benefice were responsible for fulfilling the functions corresponding to that benefice. But soon it became common to hold a benefice *sine cura*—from which the English word "sinecure" derives—that is, "without care," without having to be bothered with pastoral or ecclesiastical responsibilities. In some cases, part of the income of the benefice was used to employ somebody to take care of the corresponding tasks, while the rest went to the absent beneficiary. This was one of the factors leading to that "pluralism" that so disgusted the reformers, Catholic as well as Protestant. If it was possible to hold a benefice without performing its duties, it was also possible to hold several benefices without fulfilling the duties of any. Frequently benefices were used in a manner similar to today's scholarships, in order to cover the expenses of a particular student, bachelor, or even professor. John Calvin himself, who later became famous as a spokesman and leader of the Protestant Reformation, was able to study thanks to the system of benefices. His father belonged to the petite bourgeoisie, and when he had to face serious economic difficulties, the entire family was taken in by an aristocratic family by the name Mommon. Calvin was able to do his first studies in company of the Mommon children. In 1521, when he was only twelve years old, he was made beneficiary chaplain of the chapel of Notre Dame de la Gélasie thanks to the intervention of the Mommon family and of the Bishop of Noyon, Calvin's native city. It was thanks to this benefice that, two years later, Calvin was able go to Paris to study with the Mommon children. Six years thereafter, Calvin's father obtained another benefice for him, so that young Calvin, besides being a beneficiary, was also pluralistic! With the income of these benefices Calvin covered the expense of his studies in Paris, Orleans, and Bruges. Finally, in 1534, after his conversion to Protestantism, he renounced both benefices.

The use of benefices or sinecures as a way to cover the expenses of students and professors contributed to the growing distance between the university and the parish. Those who studied in the university thanks to benefices seldom did it in order to prepare to fulfill the functions of the benefices they enjoyed. On the contrary, the benefice itself, being permanent, allowed them to continue studying indefinitely. In such circumstances, whether such studies were relevant to the religious lives of the people or not was not a question to cause great concern to either students or professors, many of whom looked down on the less educated clergy who fulfilled the duties of their benefices.

This distance between church and academia became greater thanks to the course followed by philosophical and theological studies from the end of the thirteenth century until well into the fifteenth. The scholastic method required that ever so subtle distinctions be made in order to be able to respond to the biblical, theological, and philosophical authorities that seemed to contradict one another. A good sign of this is that, while Bonaventure and Thomas Aquinas in the middle of the thirteenth century were called the doctors "Seraphic" and "Angelic," in the following century John Duns Scotus (ca. 1265–1308) received the title of "Subtle Doctor." Toward the end of the fourteenth century and early on the fifteenth the most famous theologians had far surpassed the subtleties of Duns Scotus. To this was added the spirit of the university itself, in which professors were encouraged to compete among themselves and rivalry came to acrimonious levels. Once again, the very method of scholasticism, with its *quaestiones disputatae* and *quaestiones de quodlibet,* fostered this rivalry, which soon made Franciscans and Dominicans argue not only with the secular teachers but also among themselves. Professors accused one another of heresy, and one of the most common forms of literature became the *correctoria,* writings in which the opinions of opponents were "corrected."

Finally, as we consider late medieval scholasticism, it is important to underscore the manner in which scholastic theology, led by its own philosophical suppositions and its method, developed an ever-growing contrast and even opposition between faith and reason. Saint Thomas had declared that there were three kinds of truths. The first kind are truths of reason, for which revelation is not necessary. The third are truths of faith, which can only be known by revelation. And in between there is an intermediate degree of truths that are both of faith and of reason, even though reason can actually reach them. These are truths necessary for salvation, and therefore God has revealed them so that even those who cannot follow the rational argument supporting them will not be lost. (For instance, God's existence can be proved rationally; but since it is necessary for salvation, it has been revealed so that no one will be lost for not being able to follow the rational proofs of God's existence.) Duns Scotus rejected this distinction, saying that there are only proofs of faith and reason. This in turn led to an increasing distance between the two so that truths of faith, being "above reason," had little or nothing to do with truths of reason. The extreme to which such tendencies led could be seen in the fourteenth and fifteen centuries in the work of William of Ockham (ca. 1310–49) and his successors, for whom the absolute power of God—the *potentia Dei absoluta*—is such that it is not subject to any logic. God is not subject to the idea of the good, since anything that God does, for the mere fact that God has done it, is good. But, thanks to God's love and mercy, God has willingly limited this power, subjecting it to a certain order of reason. This limited power of God—the *potentia Dei ordinata*—is the reason why there is a predictable order in creation. The fact that two and two are four is the result of the manner in which God has ordered things; but God could very well have determined that two and two would make five, or three.

The net result of this growing contrast between faith and reason was a parallel distance between the academy and the parish. If reason is not related to faith, what profit can studying be for those who are to minister to the faith of the believers?

How are we to judge this scholasticism of the late Middle Ages? Some have called it the "autumn" of the Middle Ages, usually meaning their decline.[5] In contrast, some point out that autumn is a fruitful time and therefore prefer to speak of "the harvest" of the Middle Ages.[6] Were those centuries the dusk of the glories of the thirteenth? Or were they the culmination? The answer to these questions depends on what one understands to be the purpose and function of theology. On the one hand, there is no doubt that the theologians of the late Middle Ages took the method and perspectives of scholasticism to their last consequences. In that sense, their work is truly a "harvest." But on the other hand, if the purpose of theology is to serve the life of the church, there are ample reasons to think that this was an "autumn," or even a "fall." Still, one must acknowledge that several of the major theologians of those last centuries of the Middle Ages were profoundly involved in the life of the church. Thus, for instance, William of Ockham defended Franciscan poverty against the papacy. And several of the main leaders of the conciliar movement, which hoped to reform the church by the convocation of a council, were academicians. Among them one may mention Marsilio of Padua, William of Ockham, and Pierre d'Ailly. But despite their involvement in such debates, the theologians of the times made little impact on the daily life of Christian believers, on the thought and pastoral practices of most of the clergy, or on devotion. This does not mean that they were not devout persons, since the study of the personal libraries of several professors shows that, at least in Germany, they were indeed concerned about their own devotions as well as their pastoral practices. But the fact remains that the shape that theology had taken made it practically unreachable for the laity as well as for most of the clergy. What took place at universities was far from the times of Bonaventure and Saint Thomas. As a scholar has said, "the scholasticism of the fourteenth and fifteenth centuries became extraordinarily heavy and boring."[7]

In summary, during the last centuries of the Middle Ages the scholasticism that had flourished in the thirteenth century was taken to its ultimate consequences, with distinctions ever more subtle and with questions ever more recondite. This led to a growing distance between the academy and the parish church, or between the academicians and common believers. The other side of the coin is that the ignorance of the clergy—particularly of those who served directly in parishes—which for quite some time had been abysmal, became even worse, now with the apparent justification that, after all, studies did not seem to lead to greater relevance for the life of believers, nor to an improvement in pastoral practices.

9
In Quest of Alternatives

The growing distance between academic theology and the religious life of the people led to initiatives that eventually would have an impact on the entire church as well as on the academy. The most notable and influential of them was the community called "Brethren of the Common Life"—and, in parallel fashion, the "Sisters of the Common Life." Its founder was Gerard (Geert) Groote, who had studied in Korr, Paris, and Prague and was supported by an ecclesiastical benefice until a profound religious experience led him to renounce it and devote himself to the life of contemplation. Seven years later he felt called to preach and soon became a famous preacher who proclaimed the divine love and attacked the corruption of the clergy. As was to be expected, he was accused of heresy. But such accusations had no foundation, for Groote was perfectly orthodox and his life was far above any suspicion. Soon he gathered around him a group of followers who took the name of "Brethren of Common Life."

Although, as their name indicates, these brethren lived in community and shared all goods, they were not monks, for they did not make permanent vows. Any who wished to abandon the community in order to follow a different path— for instance, to work in a trade, marry and have a family, and so forth—could do this without any recrimination. Shortly after his conversion, probably about the year 1375, Groote wrote his *Resolutions and Intentions, but not Vows*, which begins by declaring:

> I intend to order my life to the glory, honor, and service of God and to the salvation of my soul; to put no temporal good of body, position, fortune, or learning ahead of my soul's salvation; and to pursue the imitation of God in every way consonant with learning and discernment and with my own body and estate, which predispose certain forms of imitation.[1]

The very title of this writing shows how Groote understood the difference between the life he proposed and monasticism. Monks and friars make permanent vows; Groote and his "brothers" and "sisters" made resolutions that allowed them to be part of a community for a time and then to leave it in order to follow a different style of life. This distinction also was a way of not presuming on one's will but rather trusting at each step on the grace of God and being open to new calls. But, even though they did not make vows, the Brethren and Sisters of the Common Life lived in monastic communities, eighteen of which were founded during Groote's lifetime—although the most famous was the one in Windesheim, founded two years after Groote's death.

The Brethren of the Common Life became known above all for their educational work and for their use of vernacular languages. When Groote began teaching in the Netherlands, ignorance reigned. Many among the clergy—including some who occupied high positions in the hierarchy—hardly knew how to read. They certainly knew no Latin, which meant that they could not read the books of authors such as Augustine, Cassiodore, Isidore, and Gregory the Great in which some of the knowledge of antiquity was preserved. In every *scriptorium* of the Brethren of Common Life, manuscripts were copied and then circulated throughout the land—and later also in Germany and beyond. Much of this production was written in the vernacular languages, in a policy that Groote himself had set by translating the Bible into Dutch. As soon as the printing press became available, the Brethren of Common Life adopted it as a way of spreading knowledge to such a point that at the end of the fifteenth century they had some sixty presses. But the means by which the Brethren of Common Life made their greatest impact was their schools.

At the beginning, the main purpose of the schools of the Brethren of the Common Life was to educate the rest of the population, and therefore the first schools were devoted to teaching the rudiments of reading and mathematics. But soon their curricula were amplified in order to include also philosophy and theology, and thus they became centers for the education of the clergy throughout the Netherlands and some regions of Germany. As a result, several of the most illustrious figures of the time were a product of the schools—among them Nicholas of Cusa, Thomas à Kempis, Erasmus, Luther, and the reforming pope Hadrian VI. And, when in 1568 Rome invited the Jesuits to propose improvements to the general practice of education, much of what the Jesuits suggested was taken from the practices and programs of the Brethren of the Common Life.

The teaching of the Brethren was very different from what took place in the universities, for it was inspired by a new form of devotion, called *devotio moderna*. The point of departure for this devotion was that all knowledge must be directed to the life of devotion and the practice of the faith. Thus, almost at its very beginning, the well-known book *Imitation of Christ*, attributed to Thomas à Kempis (ca. 1379–1471), a member of the Brethren, declares:

> What avail is it to a man to reason about the high, secret mysteries of the Trinity if he lack humility and so displeases the Holy Trinity? Truly, it avails nothing. Deeply inquisitive reasoning does not make a man holy or righteous, but a good life makes him beloved by God. I would rather feel compunction of heart for my sins than merely know the definition of compunction....All that is in the world is vanity except to love God and to serve Him only. This is the most noble and the most excellent wisdom that can be in any creature: by despising the world to draw nearer and nearer to the kingdom of heaven.[2]

And then the same author puts in the mouth of Jesus the following words:

> My son, says our Lord, do not let fair and subtle words move you, for the kingdom of heaven does not stand in words, but in good, virtuous works. Give heed to My words, for they inflame the heart and enlighten the understanding; they bring compunction of heart for sins past, and oftentimes cause great heavenly comfort to come into the soul. Never read any science to the end that you may be called wise. Study, rather, to mortify in yourself, as much as possible, all stirring of sin; that will be more profitable to you than the knowledge of many hard or subtle questions.[3]

The *devotio moderna* reflected in these expressions was different from two earlier forms of devotion. One was devotion of the "schools"—that is, of scholasticism—in which knowledge seemed to be confused with devotion and obedience. The other was a series of beliefs and practices that were common among the unlearned and which the Brothers of the Common Life considered superstitions: omens, prophecies, private visions, the constant search and claim of miracles, and so forth. Instead of these two, the *devotio moderna* proposed a life of persistent discipline whose purpose was, by imitating Christ, to become more like him. But at the same time the *devotio moderna* underscored the need for moderation as part of that very discipline and rejected the apparently heroic asceticism of some of the monastic traditions as well as of some popular movements such as the flagellants, for whom bodily punishment was part of true religion. The discipline that the *devotio moderna* proposed included study. But that was not study in order to be able to boast of knowing more than others, but study leading to greater dedication to the subject being studied, that is, God. It was also a profoundly christocentric pursuit with a strong emphasis on the study of the scripture—although, once again, the purpose of such study was not to know scripture better but better to conform to it. For this reason, the *devotio moderna* proposed method and discipline in study as well as in all of life. Such method and discipline would lead to the knowledge of God. And this knowledge would not be only intellectual but also affective, so that the very character of the person would be shaped after the character of God. Thus, while there was stress on the need for a moral and even moderately ascetic life, what was most important in such a life was "inwardness"—what took place within the person—and not any external manifestation of piety or devotion, for such manifestations are valid only if they are true expressions of inwardness.

The Brethren of the Common Life made a great impact on basic education—so much so, that the practice of dividing elementary education into eight grades, still prevalent in many places, has its roots in their work. They also limited the use of physical punishment as a means of teaching and established the practice of employing the more advanced students as tutors for the younger ones.

When their programs were amplified in order to include theology, the same methods resulted in a system of mentors that produced a large number of priests formed in the schools of the Brethren of the Common Life. These priests practiced *devotio moderna* and employed the teaching methods they had learned from the Brethren.

It is also important to point out that, in spite of the emphasis on moderation and discipline and of the rejection of "superstitions," the *devotio moderna*, in its critique of the intellectual elitism of the schools, provided the background for popular movements that, particularly in the sixteenth century, would claim to be based on private revelations and knowledge given to the unlearned but hidden to the rest. Thus, in the *Imitation of Christ* one reads: "I am He who also suddenly illuminates and lifts up a humble soul, so that it can take and receive in short time the true reason of the wisdom of God more perfectly than another who studies ten years in the schools and lacks humility."[4]

The most famous of the many thinkers who were formed under the wing of the Brethren of the Common Life was Desiderius Erasmus of Rotterdam (1469–1536), who under the Brethren had become acquainted with the new humanistic currents of his time. Humanism was a movement that expanded throughout Western Europe under the impulse of two important events. The first of these was the invention of the movable type printing press, which made it possible for scholars to have access to a greater number of books, as well as to make their ideas and work known to a wider circle of colleagues scattered throughout Europe. The second was the fall of Constantinople, which was taken by the Turks in 1453, with the result that many Greek-speaking scholars took refuge in Western Europe, bringing not only their language but also a vast number of Greek manuscripts until then unknown in the West. Supported by these events, humanism devoted itself to the cultivation of letters, particularly in imitation of classical letters, both Greek and Latin. The study of Greek, which until that point had been very limited in the Latin West, became more generalized. Now in possession of different versions of ancient texts—including the Bible—scholars devoted their time to the hard and meticulous task of seeking to restore the original text of works that had arrived to them in manuscripts that did not always agree among themselves—what was eventually called "textual criticism." This was done also with the New Testament, which the humanists now began studying in its original Greek and also with the Old Testament, for there soon were Christian scholars who learned Hebrew and began reading the biblical text in that language—and whom often the more conservative accused of being "judaizers." In Spain, the most able representative of these new trends was Cardinal Francisco Jiménez de Cisneros, who founded the University of Alcalá de Henares with the purpose of promoting humanistic studies and directed the compilation of the famous Complutensian (after *Complutum*, the Latin name for Alcalá) Polyglot Bible, which included both the Greek and Hebrew texts.

But Erasmus was widely acknowledged as the leader of the movement, to the point that he came to be known as "the prince of humanists." Thanks to the influence of the Brethren of the Common Life and of the *devotio moderna*, Erasmus was convinced that the best way to know the Christian faith was not the speculations and debates of scholasticism but rather the work and teachings of Jesus himself, as well as of the ancient "Fathers" of the church. This was one of the main reasons leading him to publish the New Testament in Greek in 1516, as well as a critical edition of the works of Jerome. This was followed by similar editions of others among the "Fathers" of the church. For this reason, while the humanists exalted him, the theologians in the University of Louvain—and soon also in other universities—responded by declaring that Latin was the best language for the study of scripture and that the best way to know and understand Christianity was the method established by the scholastics.

Following the example of the Brethren of the Common Life, Erasmus took an interest in the education of children. In 1529 he published *De pueris insistituendi—On the education of children*—where he proposed new methods of teaching that were based on his vision of childhood, not as part of a fully corrupt humanity but rather as the promise of a new and better humanity. For this reason he rejected physical punishment and declared that if children did not learn, this was to be laid at the feet of the poor educational practices of their teachers.

In 1518 Erasmus published a treatise *De ratio verae theologiae—On the reason [or order] of true theology*. There he rejected the common opinion that theological studies should be grounded on logic and speculative theology and proposed that instead one should begin by the study of the classical languages—Latin, Greek, and Hebrew—as well as of history and moral philosophy. The purpose of such studies should be to enable the student to practice critical judgment, a moral life, and the careful study of scripture and of the "Fathers" of the church. According to Erasmus, the new pastors and other church leaders that would be the outcome of this program of studies would lead to a renewal of the church, whose corruption Erasmus had attacked in 1515 in his *Adagia*. He saw the church as plagued by superstition, by leaders quite ready to bow to the desires of the powerful—desires that often led to unnecessary wars—by corrupt popes and bishops, by ignorant priests, and by theologians who spent their time in vain speculations. In response to that situation, it was necessary to recover the simple Christianity, the profound faith, and the moral fiber reflected in the New Testament and in the lives and writings of the "Fathers" of the church.

In summary, partly as a reaction to the apparently useless and even corrupting subtleties of late scholasticism, and partly as a response to the reigning corruption and ignorance, there were movements such as the Brethren of the Common Life and the humanists following Erasmus that proposed a new devotion and new methods, programs, and institutions of study. These programs of study, although originally not addressed directly at pastoral and ministerial education, soon left their mark on a new generation of scholars and students who were very different from the scholastics, as well as on a growing number of pastors and church leaders for whom it was impossible to separate study from devotion and the practice of charity.

10
The Protestant Reformation

When we come to the sixteenth century and the Protestant Reformation, one must begin by remembering that the Reformation itself began in a university environment, and it was the universities that provided its most important leaders for several generations. Martin Luther, a priest and an Augustinian monk, was above all a university professor. His vision of justification by grace was the result of the meeting of his own spiritual anguish and his studies of the Bible—studies that he undertook not only for devotional reasons but also as a way to prepare his lectures at the University of Wittenberg. From April 1515 to September 1516, Luther lectured on the Epistle to the Romans, and almost immediately he began another series on Galatians. As we read the commentaries Luther wrote at the time, one can see in them the foundation of what took place on the well-known date of October 31, 1517, and its aftermath. And, even after that great protest, and in the midst of all the disturbances and conflicts that it produced, practically until the very end of his days Luther continued being a university professor and lecturer.

But Luther himself knew that his gifts were not those best conducive to providing for the continuation and permanence of his reforming work. Those were rather the gifts of his young colleague and friend Phillip Melanchthon, as Luther himself declared:

> I am born to fight against innumerable monsters and devils. I must remove stumps and stones, cut away thistles and thorns, and clear the wild forests, and Master Philippus come along softly and gently, sowing and watering with joy, according to the gifts which God has abundantly bestowed upon him.[1]

Thus, as we deal with the matter of ministerial education within the context of the Reformation, our attention must not focus on Luther, but rather on Melanchthon, who joined the faculty of the University of Wittenberg in 1518, less than a year after the episode of Luther's Ninety-Five Theses, and remained there until his death in 1560.

The University of Wittenberg had been founded in 1502 and therefore was still in its formative stages. Melanchthon had not been the original candidate of choice for his prospective colleagues—including Martin Luther—who preferred a more experienced professor. But four days after his arrival at the city, Melanchthon gave his first public lecture, *On the Correction of Studies for Youth*, and the reaction was one of surprised approval. Shortly thereafter Luther wrote a common friend about Melanchthon, telling him that "on the fourth day after his arrival he delivered a most learned and chaste oration and there was so much applause and admiration on every side that you need not now commend him to us."[2] In that speech Melanchthon reviewed the history of studies from classical and biblical antiquity, arguing that with the course of time the ancient truths and knowledge had been lost, with the result that, in the field of religion, the message of the Bible had been hidden by a collection of "human solutions, ceremonies, and commentaries."[3] But now one could see in the University of Wittenberg the beginning of a new way of reading scripture and teaching its truths and the promise of a new dawn. This new method must forsake the practices and traditions of scholasticism, with its vain subtleties, and go directly to the original sources, both of classical antiquity and of Christianity. In other words, Melanchthon was joining the humanist theme of a "return to the sources," particularly to the authority of scripture and Jesus Christ, and he therefore insisted that the study of Hebrew, Greek, and Latin should be at the very heart of the curriculum. (One may note that Melanchthon was a grandnephew to Johannes Reuchlin, who for years had been involved in a bitter controversy with the Dominicans, who accused him of heresy and "judaizing" because he studied and proposed the study of Hebrew.) It was also necessary to emphasize the liberal arts, which in Melanchthon's mind had been neglected. The reason for all this should not be mere curiosity, but better to know Christ and his truth. And, according to the proposal of the young professor, this new education should be institutionalized both in the educational curriculum and in the organization of the schools themselves.

Thus began Phillip Melanchthon's long teaching career. Thanks to the fame and work of Luther and the publications both of the Reformer and of other professors who supported him, but also to the renown of Phillip Melanchthon himself, soon the University of Wittenberg became the center of Reformation, where those who sought to prepare for the work of reforming the church went to study. When Melanchthon arrived at the university, its total enrollment was one hundred and twenty students. Two years later, attendance at his lectures reached six hundred—and, according to some witnesses, even two thousand.

The work of Melanchthon in the field of education, both general and theological, was such that he was given the title that before had been reserved for Hrabanus Maurus: *Preaceptor Germaniae*—Teacher of Germany. This work took two parallel directions. The first was writing and publishing an entire series of texts that were soon employed throughout Germany. The second was the reformation of the educational system itself. As to the textbooks, Melanchthon's production, and its reach and impact, were surprising. He was twenty-one years old when he published a Greek grammar that he revised several times, which continued being the basic textbook for the study of that language throughout Germany at least until the middle of the seventeenth century. His Latin grammar was even more long lived, for it was employed at least until the eighteenth century. In order to understand the importance of such a grammar, it is necessary to remember that Latin, although no one's native language, was the common language that scholars—and sometimes also merchants—employed in order to communicate among themselves beyond the barriers resulting from the multitude of languages that they spoke. In the case of theological studies, Latin allowed teachers and students from various countries to study together—which gave university studies an international nature and at the same time contributed to the diffusion of Protestant ideas and teachings.

While rejecting the sterile rationalism of medieval scholasticism, Melanchthon insisted on the value of rational thought, and to this end he wrote a manual of logic. He also wrote an entire series of books to serve as introductions to history, physics, psychology, and theology.

All of these books—and many others that his colleagues, friends, and disciples produced thanks to his support and inspiration—were to serve as the foundation for an entire educational program, which began at the elementary school and went on through university. This program, which Melanchthon proposed in his first university lecture, was the inspiration for the *Letter to the Councilmen of All the German Cities*, which Luther wrote in 1524 and in which he proposed that the government should establish public schools. This in turn led to the basic plan of studies that Melanchthon proposed in 1528, which became the foundation for the creation of public schools.

As to the university level, Melanchthon's reformation, as he proposed in his initial speech and was soon embodied in Wittenberg, quickly expanded to other university centers. At the University of Wittenberg itself, Melanchthon proposed a new theological curriculum in which teaching would be grounded, not in the philosophical scholasticism of earlier generations but in biblical study based on solid exegesis in the original languages. This curriculum was adopted by

71

the university in 1533. It also required ample knowledge of classical letters, both Greek and Latin. As to biblical studies, Melanchthon proposed beginning with the study of Romans, then moving to the rest of the New Testament, then to the Old Testament, and finally to seal the entire process with the careful study of the Gospel of John. For theology itself, he suggested a program of studies based on the logical and historical order of various subjects, so that one would begin with the doctrine of God, then move to creation, sin, redemption, law and gospel, and so on, ending with eschatology.

Melanchthon's work on university reformation was not limited to Wittenberg. Since at that time many universities were being founded, Melanchthon was able to participate actively in the formation of several of them—in Greifswald, Königsberg, Jena, and Marburg—besides contributing to the revision of curricula in others—among them, Köln, Tübingen, Leipzig, and Heidelberg. (Regarding the latter, where he himself had studied, Melanchthon had commented that what was taught there was much trivia as well as...more trivia!)

Melanchthon's vast vision of the educational task, which included everything from primary school to the most advanced studies, is summarized in his following words, taken from *School Order for the Schools of Mecklenburg*, published in 1552. There he affirms that

> He Himself [God] wrote the Ten Commandments on tables of stone and gave commandment that the books of the prophets and apostles should be read and learned.... Since it is from these books that doctrine is to be learned, it is highly necessary that there be those who can read. And whoever is to teach others must himself be familiar with the entire substance of the doctrine and must know where and how all the articles in the Holy Scriptures support and explain one another. In order that there be certainty in the interpretation of the Holy Scriptures, there must be many who understand the language of the prophets and apostles and who can give information and testimony from their thorough understanding. In a word, whoever is to teach others properly must be prepared through the arts which are of service in that work.[4]

Since Melanchthon's purpose was to return to the sources in order to know Christ better, the biblical and theological disciplines were always prominent in his vision of the entire educational program. At all levels education should seek not only to study the subject matter at hand but also to create virtue and to lead the students to understand and live the faith more fully. Naturally, this meant that the apex of the entire program, as a necessary element crowning the rest, was theological and ministerial education.

It is within this context that we must understand two of Luther's most widely read writings in the sixteenth century, his *Greater Catechism* and his *Lesser Catechism*—both written in 1529 and therefore produced within the context of the educational plan proposed by Melanchthon, which Luther enthusiastically supported. These two catechisms set the norm for the following centuries, for they were printed for the use of the public at large, and were among the first documents so produced. They were parallel, for they followed the same order of discussion: The Ten Commandments, the Creed, the Lord's Prayer, baptism, and Communion. The *Lesser Catechism* was for children, and Luther expected that it would be taught not only in church but also at home by parents. The latter were to attend the church in order to learn there the *Greater Catechism*, which would serve both for their own lives and for the task of teaching the *Lesser Catechism* to their children—although in fact the *Greater Catechism* was written before the lesser and therefore had an independent existence. All of this was possible thanks to the printing press, of which Luther made greater use than any theologian before him.

Melanchthon's interest in ministerial education became particularly pressing after the "visitations" of 1527. After much pleading and suggestions on Luther's part, the elector John of Saxony—whose capital was Wittenberg—ordered that a series of visits to the churches and schools of the entire area be conducted in order to make certain that they were fulfilling their mission, that their accounts and administration were in order, and that the true doctrine of the gospel was being taught. These visits were entrusted to commissions that included pastors, professors, and people of administrative skills. Melanchthon was part of a commission visiting Thuringia. He was overwhelmed by what he saw. Many priests and monks had accepted the faith of the Reformation simply because they were told to do so and had no idea of the doctrinal points on which Protestants differed from Roman Catholicism. Some did not understand justification by faith and therefore preached an antinomian interpretation, which could well lead to libertinism. Economic and sexual corruption, as well as doctrinal errors, were quite common. There were some schoolteachers who did not even know how to read but had simply memorized some of the fundamental texts such as the Creed, the Ten Commandments, and the Lord's Prayer.

The result of that experience, which was shared by others among the visitors, was an entire educational program that the University and the Elector approved in 1528 and which was then published under the title *Instructions for the Visitors of Parish Pastors in Electoral Saxony*. Although this document frequently appears among Luther's writings, it is generally agreed that its main author was Melanchthon. The first part of the *Instructions* was a summary of Christian doctrine as it was to be taught in parishes and schools. This includes frequent doctrinal warnings, such as that it is necessary to preach penance, and to punish fearless behavior which is now in the world and has it origins, at least in part, in a wrong understanding of the faith. For many who hear that they should believe, so that all their sins will be forgiven, fashion their own faith and think they are pure.[5]

But above all the document offers a positive exposition of the main points of doctrine under subjects such as "The Doctrine," "The Ten Commandments," "The True Prayer," "The Tribulation," and so forth. The second part offers the plan of studies that has already been outlined. And—what is of greater interest for our subject—he insists on the need for theological education, "for...some suppose it is sufficient if the preacher can read German, but this is a dangerous delusion. For whoever would teach another must have long practice and special ability which are achieved only after long study from youth on....For it is not an insignificant art to teach others clearly and correctly, and it is not within the power of such folk as have no learning."[6]

The result of all of this was a growing insistence on the need to widen the scope of theological education. Up to that point, it was ordination that made one a pastor or priest, and studies were not particularly necessary. But by the middle of the sixteenth century it became normal for candidates to the Lutheran ministry to study at universities where they pursued theological studies and prepared for the task of teaching the people. Such studies became more necessary since now pastors and other church leaders not only had to teach the people much they had not known before but also had to know how to face Catholic opponents who called them heretics and were armed with a series of elaborate arguments. In consequence, there was an astonishing and even explosive growth in the student population not only in Wittenberg but also in other Protestant universities.

The educational work of the illustrious *Praeceptor Germaniae* had an enormous impact. Hundreds of young men committed to the Reformation movement and to seeking greater knowledge and better instruments to serve in parishes and schools flocked to the University of Wittenberg and others.

Furthermore, inspired by Melanchthon's work, several other educators and theologians sought to develop a theological curriculum that was more ordered and complete. Foremost among them is Andreas Hyperius (1511–64), who in 1556 proposed the division of the curriculum into three parts: (1) the study of the Bible and its interpretation, (2) doctrinal or "positive" theology, and (3) more practical studies, which would be concerned with ecclesiastical administration and governance, preaching, and worship and rites. This division that Hyperius suggested was very similar to what eventually most Protestant seminaries would follow. It is important to point out that Hyperius wrote the first Protestant treatise on homiletics, *De formandis concionibus sacris—On the shaping of sacred speeches.*

At approximately the same time as Melanchthon, Bullinger, Zwingli's successor in Zürich, was proposing similar reforms. He, too, was convinced that the theological curriculum should include both classical literature and the biblical and classical languages—Latin, Greek, and Hebrew, to be studied in that order—as well as the writings of the most prestigious ancient Christian writers, particularly Saint Augustine. But Bullinger laid more emphasis than Melanchthon on the context of these studies and constantly underscored the need of piety and devotion in the theological task. Also, since his own background was Cistercian, Bullinger proposed the manner in which the lives of students should be ordered, with some hours dedicated to study, others to devotion, and so forth. Likewise in Strasbourg, Jean Strum created and for forty-three years led a "gymnasium" or academy along similar lines.

However, it was the Academy of Geneva that soon came to occupy among the Reformed—that is, among Calvinists—a place similar to that of University of Wittenberg in the formation of the first Lutheran leaders. Like Melanchthon, Calvin exerted his influence through two main means: his writings and the program of studies that he designed for Geneva.

As is well known, the most important among Calvin's writings was *Institutes of the Christian Religion*, published first as a pocketbook—although a book for the rather ample pockets of that time! But it progressively grew to the point that it was four fairly large volumes. On the reasons that led him to write the *Institutes*, twenty years later Calvin said that he had originally written this book in order to refute the lies of those who accused Protestants of all sorts of errors.[7] But as years went by and Calvin added new sections in which he summarized and discussed various controversies that emerged, that fairly small book became a vast treatise of Protestant theology, and soon it became the most influential of all Protestant writings, as well as the preferred textbook in universities and schools of theology not only in Switzerland but also in parts of Germany as well as in the Netherlands, Hungary, and the British Isles.

The *Catechism* that Calvin published in 1542 was clearly inspired by similar earlier writings by Luther and Martin Bucer. It was not addressed to leaders in the church but to the laity in general. On Sunday afternoons, for parents and children, there was preaching devoted to a question in the catechism that was to be studied that week, thus clearly connecting preaching with the education of believers. Also, for many years Calvin commented publicly on the various books of the Bible, and his fame grew to such an extent that soon theologians and students from other regions came to learn from these lectures. Those commentaries were then published and widely used by Calvinist preachers. Through such writings, Calvin left an indelible imprint on theological formation within the Reformed tradition.

From an early date, Calvin was concerned for programs and institutions for theological education. In the *Ecclesiastical Ordinances* of 1541, he established, besides the offices of pastor, elder, and deacon, that of "doctor." There he says:

> The proper function of doctors is to teach the faithful the correct doctrine, so that the purity of the gospel is not corrupted either by ignorance or by evil opinions. . . . They are the aids and instruments necessary to preserve the church from the desolation of the lack [*manque*, which may mean either the shortcomings or the scarcity] of pastors and ministers. In order to use an easily understood word, we shall call this the order of the schools.
>
> A lecture on theology in which he [the doctor] deals with both the Old and the New Testaments is the function that is closest to the ministry and government of the church.
>
> But, since one cannot profit from such lessons without first being instructed in the human languages and sciences, . . . it would be necessary to create a school to instruct them, preparing them both for the ministry and for the civil government.[8]

In these *Ordinances*, approved by the City Council of Geneva, Calvin expressed a desire that did not come to fruition until eighteen years later. Although the Council approved the plan, it would not set aside funds for its implementation. Therefore Calvin had to find support among private donors. Finally, on June 5, 1559, Calvin presided over the ceremony opening the Academy. It is interesting to note that, while the City Council of Geneva would not allot the funds necessary to establish the school that Calvin had proposed, Bern did provide the resources for a school in nearby Lausanne where Calvinist theology was taught. The Rector of the new school in Geneva was Theodore Beza, who had earlier held a similar post in Lausanne. Calvin had prepared a system of government as well as the outline of a program of studies for the Academy, and Beza's task was to implement them. These plans would include a *schola privata* and a *schola publica*. In the first, reading and writing would be taught, at first in Latin and French and then in Greek. The curriculum for this school would also include the liberal arts. The *schola publica* would be a more advanced school where courses would be offered on theology and exegesis—normally by means of lectures on those subjects.

In 1564, five years after the founding of the Academy, Beza would tell Bullinger that there were twelve hundred students in the *schola publica* and three hundred in the *privata*. Among those three hundred there were several who would soon take Calvinism to the Netherlands, Scotland, and England—countries where schools and programs would soon be established following the Genevan model.

The early leaders of the radical reformation were highly educated. Before joining the reformation movement, Conrad Grebel had studied at the universities of Basel, Vienna, and Paris. Later, when joining a group of studies that Zwingli led in Zürich, he became known for his studies on classical Greek literature, as well as for his work on the biblical text, both in Hebrew and in Greek. Balthasar Hubmaier studied at the University of Fribourg, and later was a professor of theology at the University of Ingolstadt, whose rector he became in 1515. Although he never attained a university degree, Caspar Schwenkfeld studied in Köln, Frankfort, and Erfurt and was proficient in Latin, Greek, and Hebrew. He employed these languages in his biblical studies and in polemics with both Catholics and other Protestants. The only one among the main leaders of that first generation who did not have formal university studies was Melchior Hoffman, who was a furrier by trade but also devoted himself to the careful study of the scriptures as well as some of the classical German mystics. Menno Simons had the typical education of a Catholic priest of his time. He therefore knew Latin, some Greek, and no Hebrew. As he himself later declared, during all the time when he "was stupid," he never read the Bible, partly because he was afraid that it might confuse him. But after his conversion to Protestantism he devoted himself to the careful study of scriptures as well as the "Fathers" of the church.

In spite of such a background, the vicissitudes that Anabaptism had to endure in its early years, particularly the persecution that it suffered, left little room for formal studies, and therefore it was much later that the heirs of that tradition began founding schools for the preparation of their leaders.

In summary, with few exceptions, the nature itself of the Protestant Reformation and of the opposition against it led the main leaders of Protestantism to stress the education of both clergy and laity. This was partly done by means of literary production that was disseminated thanks to the recently invented printing press and partly through educational institutions and programs. The main examples of these institutions are the University of Wittenberg for the Lutheran tradition and the Academy of Geneva for the Reformed. Such was the success of these institutions that soon formal theological studies became a requirement for ordination—which had never been the case at any point in the history of the church and would now become the norm for many churches at least until the twenty-first century.

11
The Catholic Reformation

The intensity of the theological debates with Protestants and the need to develop some arguments and to gather correct information for such debates led to a process of renewal of theological education within the Roman Catholic Church. Also, as in the case of Protestantism, Catholicism felt the impact of the interest of the humanists in the study and the cultivation of letters. This Catholic emphasis on theological formation was coupled with a new emphasis in the education of youth, and therefore theological education became part of an entire new emphasis on education, secular as well as biblical and theological.

Even so, the state of religious instruction in Catholic countries was deplorable, as may be seen in the sporadic efforts to improve it. Thus, for instance, in Milan in 1536 Father Castellino da Castello invited the children in the neighborhood to attend the catechism, rewarding them with an apple each day. This led to the birth of a confraternity devoted to the doctrinal instruction of children. But even such meager efforts were suppressed by ecclesiastical authorities, and it was only ten years later, in 1546, that da Castello's *Confraternity of Christian Doctrine* was able to work with the official support of the church.

This does not mean that there were no movements of educational reform before and apart from the Protestant challenge. Efforts had already been made by Cardinal Francisco Jiménez de Cisneros in Spain—efforts that led, among other things, to the foundation of the University of Acalá de Henares and the publication of the Complutensian Polyglot Bible. Furthermore, the voluntary or forced addition of millions of inhabitants in the New World to the Catholic Church forced missionaries to pay more attention to their catechetical instruction.

This emphasis, as well as a parallel emphasis on the wider education of priests, took official form in the Council of Trent (1545–63). In its fifth session (1546), that council dictated that each cathedral should have programs for the instruction of clergy and of those among the poor who were not able to cover the cost of their studies. This program should include the teaching of "grammar"—that is, elementary school—and "Sacred Scriptures"—meaning not only the Bible but also doctrine and theology.

Shortly thereafter, Saint Ignatius Loyola, who had always been profoundly interested in education, founded in Rome the *Collegium Germanicum*, whose purpose was to instruct young German candidates for orders. Such students obviously had to be trained for a ministry of opposition to and refutation of Protestantism. The importance of Loyola and the Society of Jesus in the entire process of academic and clerical renewal in the Catholic Church is enormous. The Jesuits were the first religious order to declare from the very beginning that one of their main occupations was education—in which one may see a reflection of the context in which the order was born, a context permeated by humanist ideas and concern over the growth of Protestantism. Even before the foundation of the *Collegium Germanicum*, the Jesuits had established schools in Spain (Candia) and Italy (in Messina and Palermo). In 1551, Ignatius wrote to his followers, encouraging them to found schools. From that time on, and until his death, each year an average of more than four schools were founded. When—for a series of political reasons that do not concern us here—the order was suppressed in 1773, it had almost eight hundred schools in which both secular subjects and ministerial preparation were offered. Almost a hundred of these were in Latin America. All of this was grounded on the *Constitutions* of the Order, whose fourth section dealt with "Teaching letters and other means by which those who join the Society are to help their neighbors." There an entire curriculum was included:

> Since the purpose of the doctrine that is learned in this Society is with divine favor to help their own souls and those of their neighbors, this will serve as a measure to determine both in general and in its particulars the matters that our members must learn, and how far they must go in them. And since generally speaking there is value in the study of humane letters in various languages, as well as of logic and philosophy, both natural and moral, of metaphysics and scholastic as well as positive theology, and sacred scripture, those who attend the schools shall study all these subjects.[1]

It was somewhat later, in 1563, that in its twenty-third session the Council of Trent took up the matter of clerical education. Its most important decision in this direction was that each diocese should provide for the training of diocesan clergy by establishing "seminaries."

Apparently, the word *seminary* was first employed in this sense seven years earlier by Cardinal Reginald Pole, who was archbishop of Canterbury during the brief restoration of Catholicism in England under the reign of Mary Tudor. In his plan for this restoration—a plan which was frustrated by the death of Mary and the accession to the throne by her half-sister Elizabeth—Pole included the founding of "seminaries" for the training of English clergy. The word *seminary* itself meant "seedbed." Therefore, what was intended was, as in a seedbed, to plant a large number of candidates, care for them in their growth process, and finally transplant them to the places where their ministry was to take place. Since Pole was an important figure in the preparation of the agenda and documents for the Council of Trent, it is not surprising that the council, when it finally came to the matter of the training of the clergy five years after Pole's death, made use of his ideas and even his vocabulary.

According to the conciliar decree, the bishops had wide latitude as to the manner in which such seminaries were to be organized. They could simply use already existent schools. Bishops of small or poor dioceses could combine their efforts with those of neighboring dioceses. Those in the larger dioceses could have more than one seminary. The council did dictate that students must be at least twelve years old, have completed their first letters, and have shown aptitude for the service of the church. In the seminary they were to be taught, besides the liberal arts, how to preach, administer the sacraments, and lead divine worship. These seminaries were different from the novitiate and from the preparation to take final vows in monastic orders, for their main purpose would be to prepare their students for diocesan priesthood. Nor were they faculties of theology like those that had existed for more than two centuries in universities for, although they would teach theology in a manner similar to universities, their purpose was not the study itself but the total formation of candidates to serve in the ordained ministry of the church.

Pope Pius IV immediately set to work on the directives of the council on theological education by naming a commission of cardinals who would direct their implementation as well as by founding the Seminary of Rome in 1565. But the most outstanding leader in this entire task was Saint Charles Borromeo, Archbishop of Milan from 1560 to 1584, who had played an important role in the Council of Trent. In Milan he made every effort to implement the dictates of the council on the founding of seminaries. Given the size of the diocese and the various existing needs, Borromeo did not found a seminary, but three. The purpose of one of them was to improve the education of those who were already ordained priests, but whose education was deficient. Another, in which the course of studies was shorter, was devoted to the training of candidates for the priesthood in rural parishes. And the third—which received most support—offered an entire course of studies that began at twelve years of age, included liberal arts and sciences, and led to a period of biblical and theological studies. Apparently,

Borromeo's purpose in founding this third seminary was to provide priests who could serve in larger parishes at a time in which many of the believers had secular studies, and also to refute the heresies that threatened Catholicism—above all, what he considered the Lutheran heresy.

The existence of various levels of education in those early seminaries soon led to the distinction between "minor seminaries," where the basic preparation needed to pursue theological studies was offered, and "major seminaries," whose curriculum focused first on philosophy and then on theology. In some cases courses offered in the universities were also used for the education of seminary students. However, the formation and spiritual guidance of these candidates to the priesthood were the responsibility of the seminaries. Therefore, the formation of these new generations of diocesan priests came to be a combination of the ancient monastic lifestyle—life in community, with established times of prayer, discipline, and so forth—with university studies. This combination of academic studies with community life was a model followed also by many modern Protestant seminaries.

Back to the Catholic Reformation of the sixteenth century and its impact on ministerial training and formation, it is necessary to insist on the importance of the Society of Jesus in the entire process. As stated above, from the very beginning that order saw education as part of its central vocation. The Jesuits studied various educational methods and institutions existing in their time, in order to take from each what could be useful. In 1584 a commission of six Jesuit scholars was convened in Rome, where they spent a year studying the best treatises on pedagogy and on the administration of schools and universities. Then followed a long series of consultations with their fellow Jesuits throughout the world. Finally, in 1599, in the name of the general of the Jesuits, the secretary of the order sent out the final text of a *Ratio studiorum*, or program of studies, which the order was to follow throughout the world, indicating that "Our comprehensive plan of education, first undertaken fourteen years ago, is now sent to all the Provinces," and "all must follow it."[2] This document established the manner in which Jesuits were to organize and lead their schools, and for a long time it would be the norm for Jesuit education as well as for that imparted in many other schools.[3]

On the organization of schools, which occupied a large part of the *Ratio*, what was proposed was an adaptation of what was known as the "Parisian method." This method—which was in fact an organizational structure rather than a pedagogical method—had become normative in several schools in Paris, due to the influence of humanism and the Brethren of the Common Life. Ignatius and most of his earlier companions had come to know that institutional organization first at the University of Alcalá—founded years earlier by Jiménez de Cisneros with the explicit purpose of following the model of Paris. Then most of those first Jesuits had gone to the University of Paris, where they saw how this manner of organizing schools functioned by focusing on the responsibilities of all the members of the university—from its professors and administrators to the students. Saint Ignatius, and then the *Ratio studiorum*, took this "method" as a principle on which to build an entire educational program.

The *Ratio* does not deal with basic studies, not because they were considered unimportant but rather because it focused its vision on programs of study beyond the basic learning of reading and writing—what was then called "grammatical studies." Therefore, the subject of the *Ratio* was what today we would call middle and higher education. That education would include liberal arts as well as philosophy and sciences and—in those schools devoted to the training of priests—theology. But according to the Parisian method this must be done in order, without mixing the various subjects and themes, thus avoiding confusion and allowing students to delve more deeply into each subject studied. For this reason the plan of studies proposed by the *Ratio*, which was dominant for centuries, consisted in three cycles or levels: the first—the "lower studies"—would normally take five years and focused on grammar, humanities, and rhetoric. The "higher studies" began the second cycle, which was a period of three years devoted to logic, mathematics, physics, ethics, and metaphysics. Finally, the third cycle, which normally took four years, was dedicated to theology—a theology based on philosophy and following the teachings of Saint Thomas Aquinas. Therefore, a young man beginning these studies at fourteen years of age could complete them at twenty-six—although, in cases of students with exceptional gifts, they were allowed to move faster along the process.

In these three cycles a pedagogical method was followed that was clearly an imitation of what Loyola and his earlier followers had seen in Paris and Alcalá. This was part of the "Parisian method," although now focusing not on the organization of the school but rather on the process of teaching itself. This method included above all the *praelectio*, in which the teacher, taking into account the work and state of knowledge of his students, would share his own, always adjusting what he said to the level of the students. The *praelectio* was followed by the "repetition"—which was not what is meant today by that word but rather a review of what had been learned. That review was constant throughout the week but was also a particular exercise on Saturday morning, when two hours were usually spent on it. Besides the *praelectio* and the repetition, the teaching method included debates and competitions among students. These were modeled after the medieval *disputationes* but had a strong dose of the humanist spirit of the sixteenth century—for several of the first Jesuits leaders criticized and even mocked the sterility of what was still being discussed in universities such as that of Paris. The *Ratio* also forbade excessive corporal punishments such as had been common until that time. And the teaching task was not limited to the actual teacher, for the more advanced students were to contribute to the teaching of the younger—in part because through teaching one learns and in part to promote solidarity among future Jesuits. In all of this, part of what was sought was that learning would be pleasant, that the curiosity of students would be stimulated, and that they would be trained for an entire life of continued study.

Another important characteristic of the curriculum that the *Ratio* established was its emphasis on the reading of classical texts—besides those on patristics and theology. Thus, for instance, at the very beginning of the plan of studies it was ordered that

> for the knowledge of language . . . daily lessons must be dedicated to teaching, among the orators, only Cicero—particularly those among his writings that deal with his moral philosophy. Among historians, Caesar, Sallustius Livius, Curtius, and others that are similar. Among the poets, Virgil, excluding the Eclogues and the fourth book of the Aeneid, as well as select texts from Horace . . . and other famous poems, although purging all of their obscenities.[4]

In this one may see two new elements that would leave their imprint on all education from that time on. The first of these is the impact of humanism. Although the Jesuits of the sixteenth century admired earlier scholasticism, humanism had led them to wish that their students know not only portions and short sayings from classical antiquity but the texts themselves. The second is the printing press, which for the first time in history made it possible for students as well as professors to have at hand full texts, and there were even sufficient copies of the same text that each student could have one. Therefore, although still some texts were read out loud in class, this was no longer done because the students had no access to them, as in the Middle Ages, but rather in order to discuss and analyze them.

The *Ratio* also prescribed a semimonastic lifestyle. The purpose of education was not only to impart information but also to lead the students to *eloquentia perfecta*—an eloquence requiring, beyond what the word means today, a character that is consonant with what has been said and taught and grounded in a profound spirituality. It is for this reason that from that moment all Catholic theological education—and not only that imparted by Jesuits—set "formation" as a goal parallel to instruction. Life in a seminary must include, beside studies, prayer and recreation. For the same reason, although it was possible for students in a seminary to pursue some of their theological studies in a nearby university or school of theology, participation in discipline and community life within the seminary could not be set aside. As to the Jesuits themselves, the practice of the

84

Spiritual Exercises of Ignatius, both before ordination and regularly thereafter, has always been a central part of their own formation, and the context within which studies are conceived and practiced.

In summary, in the history of theological education within the context of the Catholic Reformation one may see entwined two of the most important aspects of that reformation: pontifical and hierarchical reformation, which was crystallized around the decrees of the Council of Trent and the educational work of the Society of Jesus. Each of these two left its mark on the other, for among the leaders who shaped the Council of Trent and its decisions there were several Jesuits through whom the interest of that order in education—particularly clerical education—left its mark on the decisions of the council regarding education, particularly on its decree regarding the foundation of seminaries in 1563. But these decisions in turn were reflected in the educational work of the Jesuits, particularly in the *Ratio studiorum* of 1599.

Considering the resulting theological education, one may see in it a combination of the ancient monastic schools with their medieval methods and the new methods and opportunities of humanism. For this reason, both in the decrees of Trent and in the *Ratio studiorum* of the Jesuits, theological education is to take place within the context of a "seminary," which is a semimonastic institution in which devotional and community life leads to the formation of the candidate for orders. Yet the rules and the organization of the schools and seminaries did not follow the model of the earlier monastic schools but rather of the universities of Paris, Alcalá, and others. Besides, the invention of the printing press and the literary interests of the humanists gave a central place to the reading and analysis of classical and patristic texts that until then were hardly accessible to most students—or even to professors. And, thanks to the work of the humanists, these ancient texts were now read in their original languages—Greek as well as Hebrew. What thus emerged was a model of theological education that continued almost unchanged until the time of the Second Vatican Council, in the twentieth century.

12
Protestant Scholasticism and Rationalism

From its very beginnings Protestant theology was grounded in the careful study of texts and doctrines. Although Luther could speak of "filthy reason," this never led him to oppose study, as long as it was done in obedience to the word of God. And even then, already in Luther's time, Melanchthon was his closest collaborator, making use of the best philological methods available in order to interpret scriptures, insisting on the need to study the biblical languages and proposing curricular reforms that would lead to a more careful and orderly study not only of scriptures but also of classical letters, philosophy, and theology. Luther was an enthusiastic supporter of Melanchthon's entire program.

Therefore, it is not surprising that soon after the first generation of reformers—and even in their lifetimes—a process of codification and organization of theological disciplines, particularly of systematic theology, was begun. Once the survival of the reformation was guaranteed, its followers felt the need to continue the process of theological systematization and institutionalization that had already begun in the works of Melanchthon and Calvin. That process turned the Bible into an arsenal from which one could draw texts—frequently with little or no connection to their context—in order to refute one's opponents, and biblical studies tended to center on such texts and on the systematization of what they seemed to say.

This tendency has been called "Protestant scholasticism." For a long time this name had pejorative undertones, giving the impression that Protestant theology had lost sight of the new freedom that Luther had gained for it and had once again become subject to canons that were very similar to those of medieval scholasticism. More recently, some studies of that particular period have attained a measure of success in vindicating Protestant scholasticism, thus alleviating the pejorative overtones of the very name, "Protestant scholasticism." There is no doubt that Protestant scholasticism was much more fruitful than we had earlier thought. But even so, the name of "scholasticism"—not now in a pejorative, but simply in a descriptive sense—does fit it well. It was a theology of the schools, that is, of the universities. Like classical scholasticism, much of it made the views of Aristotelian philosophy and logic essential instruments. Like classical scholasticism, Protestant theology in the seventeenth century and a good part of the eighteenth sought to find an appropriate place for everything, much as the ancient medieval cathedrals. Therefore, several of the leading figures of Protestant scholasticism produced systematic works that in their thoroughness and in their length could well rival the *Summa Theologica* of Thomas Aquinas. Protestant scholasticism, like its classical counterpart, paid attention to every theological detail, no matter how unimportant or uninteresting.

However, Protestant scholasticism, like every theology, must be evaluated within the context in which it was forged. Politically, this was the time of the Thirty-Years War, a period of revolution in England, wars of religion in France, and many other events that tended to divide nations and groups and exaggerate differences and contrasts. Theologically, it was a time of debates within each of the main Protestant traditions, among those traditions themselves, and most of all with Roman Catholicism.

Within the main Protestant traditions—Lutheran and Reformed—there were soon debates regarding the legacy of the earlier reformers. In the case of Lutheranism, the main issue was a series of controversies between "Philippists"—that is, followers of Philipp Melanchthon—and "strict Lutherans." The first were more inclined to follow the irenic and mediating tendencies of Melanchthon, while the latter insisted on the most extreme positions of Luther—even though Luther himself had repeatedly endorsed the attitude and work of Melanchthon. This eventually led to the *Formula of Concord* of 1577, which set the limits of orthodox Lutheranism. Among the Reformed, similar debates—although in this case having to do with grace and predestination—led to the canons of Dort (1618–19) and to the *Confession of Westminster* (1647), which proclaimed a strict Calvinism and excluded Arminians from the ranks of Calvinists. Between the Lutherans and Reformed, there were controversies having to do mostly with the presence of Christ in Communion. On this point too Luther had been rather positive toward what Calvin had written. But now the more strict Lutherans declared that not only all Calvinists but also many Lutherans were heretics who they dubbed *cryptocalvinists*—that is, secret followers of Calvin. About the debates between Protestants on one side and Catholics on the other, it should suffice to say that such debates were constant features in the theological landscape for centuries—and in some parts of the world, even today. In these debates, Protestants found themselves needing to refute very carefully developed arguments—particularly those proposed by Robert Bellarmine—and an entire view of the history of the church proposed by Cesar Baronius, who claimed that Catholicism was the original and true church and Protestantism was a historical aberration. At about the same time, the first scientific discoveries of modernity cast doubt on much of the traditional world vision and doctrine, both Catholic and Protestant, which by reaction often resulted in more emphasis on those traditional views.

Given such contexts, is not surprising that some Protestant theologians in the late sixteenth century and into the eighteenth paid attention to every detail of doctrine and at the same time developed theological methods based on Aristotelian logic, which was generally seen as the foundation of rational thought. Therefore, extensive works such as the *Loci Theologici* by Johann Gerhard (1582–1637), which in its final edition comprised twenty-three volumes, or the *System of Theological Themes* by Abraham Calov (1612–86), in twelve volumes, were simply the result of a strong commitment to their authors' cause and an attempt to refute every argument against their views as well as to preempt any possible doubt.

All of this led Protestant scholasticism to pay particular attention to theological education. For the first time in the entire history of the church constant efforts were made so that as many as possible among the ordained ministry would have formal theological studies leading to a profound understanding of the gospel, as well as the instruments necessary to serve as shepherds of the flock. This led to a theological education that was more careful and strict, and whose curriculum was more clearly organized—much of which fulfilled the earlier wishes of Andreas Hyperius.

The concern for theological education may be seen in the work of Johann Heinrich Alsted (1588–1638), who wrote most extensively on this subject but who was only one among many who could be mentioned. Alsted was at the same time a man of encyclopedic knowledge and a convinced Calvinist who took part in the discussions of Dort.[1] His interest lay in relating all knowledge with biblical revelation, as may be seen in his later work *Encyclopaedia Biblica*. But it is in his *Logica Theologica* that Alsted deals most carefully with pastoral formation. As earlier writers, Alsted proposes a calendar that is to rule the days, months, and years of the life of students—a calendar that includes annual examinations in July, but no days of rest. As to the curriculum itself, Alsted divides it into two main headings: theory and practice. The theological disciplines include the study of doctrine—that is, theology itself—the scientific analysis of scripture, polemics, and history of theology. On the practical side, Alsted underscores homiletics and what he calls "cases of conscience" in which he studies how the pastor is to lead the flock in moral matters—and therefore includes some of what today is studied under ethics and some of the issues now discussed under pastoral care. On each of these various subjects, the student needs to read twelve books a year from beginning to end and interpret each of them analytically.

As to educational method, Alsted proposed that each subject be studied and discussed from various points of view and using various methodologies. Thus, for instance, when it comes to the matter of God, one could begin by the theological affirmation of the existence and nature of God. But this should be accompanied by an exegetical dimension, exploring and analyzing the biblical texts having to do with the subject itself, and always on the basis of the original languages. One would then move to debatable questions, to polemics, and to a global vision of what these biblical texts say, and how the whole can be brought into one.

Alsted, like all the main theologians of the time, was convinced that good theology—and therefore good theological education—was to be based on scriptures and must also have practical relevance. On the matter of the scriptural foundation of theology, he followed the general lines of the earlier reformers, and therefore he had little new to say. But it is important to mention this, for it has often been thought that Protestant scholastics, in order to build their great systems, paid more attention to logic and to intellectual consistency than to scripture. This is not true, at least not of the main theologians of the time. Thus, François Turretin (1623–87) declared that—in spite of what Saint Thomas and other medieval scholastics had affirmed—theology is not a science, for science is grounded on reason, and theology is grounded on biblical revelation.[2] If Protestant scholasticism may be accused of rationalism, in the worst of cases it is a rationalism that takes biblical revelation as its starting point and builds upon it rational arguments in order to refute those who propose different positions.

This is why in all the many curricula for theological studies that Protestant scholasticism produced, the basic study, beyond the very first letters and other foundational courses, has to do with biblical languages, as well as with principles of exegesis and interpretation.

On the practical dimension of theological studies, Gerhard affirms that theological studies must be practical, enabling anyone who is gifted by God with special power to "teach the Word of God, administer the Sacraments, and preserve ecclesiastical discipline, in order to bring about the conversion and salvation of people and to spread the glory of God."[3] This was a foundational principle in the book *Theorico-practical Theology* by the Dutchman Peter van Mastricht (1630–1706). In it, the discussion of each subject begins with a careful exegetical study of the relevant biblical passages, in order then to move to the polemical aspects of the subject and to conclude with a wide exposition on the importance of the subject for the life of the believer, both in matters of morals and in matters of devotion.

Lastly, before moving to the rationalism that became the counterpart of scholasticism, it is important to point out that English Puritanism drank from the wells of Protestant scholasticism and became its British—and later North American—expression. The Puritans proposed to organize the theological curriculum, which was then leading to a university bachelor's degree, around the biblical and scholarly languages (that is, Latin, Hebrew, and Greek) and therefore around the study of exegesis and scripture. To these were added, as in the case of continental scholasticism, an emphasis on the liberal arts and their use for polemical purposes. Finally, rhetoric had a prominent place in the curriculum, for the practical purpose of theological studies was to lead the congregation to a clearer understanding of scripture, to the improvement of behavior on biblical foundations, and to the practice of piety.[4]

This model of theological studies, which British Puritans took from Protestant scholasticism, was also the model that led to the foundation of the first school of theology in what is today the United States when, barely six years after their arrival, the Mayflower "Pilgrims" took steps to found the school of theology that eventually gave rise to Harvard University. Several others among the first North American universities had similar beginnings. And this in turn left its imprint on Protestant theological education to this day.

At the very time when Protestant scholasticism was flourishing, modern rationalism was taking its first steps. This rationalism tended to be inimical to Protestant scholasticism as well as to much traditional theology. Naturally, it is impossible to determine an exact date of the birth of modern rationalism. However, a few dates suffice to show that, as the seventeenth century advanced, so did rationalism. René Descartes was born in 1596 and, as he himself says, his great metaphysical "discovery" took place in 1619 (the same year the Synod of Dort met). His *Discourse on Method*, one of the most influential works in the development of rationalism, was published in 1637. It is not necessary to review here the entire Cartesian system. Let it suffice to say that, as a methodological principle, Descartes began by doubting all that he was unable to prove by clearly rational means. Although on the basis of that method Descartes came to affirm the existence of both God and the soul, the method itself cast doubts on the authority of scripture, which was fundamental for Protestants, as well as on the authority of the church, which was equally fundamental for Roman Catholics. From that time on, much of the work of Protestant scholasticism—as well as many of the efforts of a number of Catholic theologians—was focused on counteracting Cartesian rationalism.

British empiricism appeared in Great Britain shortly after the impact of Descartes on continental philosophy. Although it had many forerunners, its main figure was John Locke (1632–1704). Locke and many of his followers were skeptical on religious matters. Like Descartes and the continental Cartesians, they did not deny the existence of God or other fundamental tenets of religion, but they did severely limit what could be said about God and rejected any authority that was not empirical—which included scripture. Soon Deism, following the guidelines drawn by Locke and other empiricists, proposed a "simplified Christianity" or a "universal religion" that was limited to subjects such as the existence of God and the soul, life after death, and rewards and punishments in that later life.

As was to be expected, many Christians rejected such attitudes, and therefore in certain circles opposition to rationalism gave new impetus to Protestant scholasticism, with its absolute certitude and its emphasis in the authority of the scripture. But there were also those who saw Deism as a means to defend the faith before the attack of other more skeptical rationalists. Therefore, their views began making headway, not only among the exceptionally educated but also among pastors and theologians who preferred it above traditional Christianity with its doctrines and above the growing agnosticism of the time. Soon there were universities and schools of theology whose teachings were deeply influenced by Deism. As we shall see, this would lead to a reaction not only against Deism but also against the schools that seemed to abandon orthodox Christianity.

The time of Protestant scholasticism and rationalism also saw the work of the outstanding educator Jan Amos Komensky (1592–1670), generally known as John Amos Comenius. Comenius was a Moravian bishop who spent most of his life in Sweden, producing and defending new methods of education, and for this reason is known as the "father of modern education." This is due mostly to his great opus *Didactica magna*, in which he proposes an entire educational plan, beginning in childhood and leading to the most advanced studies. Also, in his *Janus linguarum reserata—The open door of languages*—published in 1631, he proposed and began publishing a series of textbooks in which he applied his educational method. This method, based on "teaching according to nature," proposed that, instead of the punishments that until then were widely employed, the motivation for study should be the natural interest and curiosity of children and youth. It is also said that Comenius was the first to publish children's books with illustrations. This is not quite true. But it is true that he was the first to use illustrations as an educational resource.

Comenius had a vision in which at least the basic level of education would be available to all, including those who labor in fields and workshops. In order to reach the more advanced levels, his plan included twenty-four years of education, always seeking the triple goal of true knowledge, true moral integrity, and true piety. These twenty-four years were to be divided into four periods: the first, on a mother's lap; the second, what he called the "vernacular school," to which all children—girls as well as boys—should attend; third, the "Latin school," which would be attended by those who instead of the more common work in the fields would be in charge of administrative specialties; and finally, university, which should be attended only by a select number of the best students, and would deal mostly with medicine, law, and theology.

Comenius had read the works of Descartes as well as of other French and British rationalists, and his positive view of humanity and its potentiality was mostly derived from them. It was this positive view that served as the foundation for his "education according to nature." This distanced him from Protestant scholasticism, Lutheran as well as Reformed, which insisted on the corruption of human nature because of sin. But at the same time some of his proposals included elements of Protestant scholasticism.

Comenius focused his attention on universal education, and therefore he paid more attention to the basic educational levels of learning than to more advanced studies—which included theology. Therefore, he never developed a curriculum for theological studies. But in his discussion of such studies one sees elements of the scholastic atmosphere of the time. Thus, for instance, the fundamental method of university studies—that is, not only of theology but also of law and medicine—would be lectures that the professor would give in the morning, followed in the afternoon by presentations on the same subject by the students, with arguments for and against a proposition. Likewise, in the final exams in the field of theology, a panel of professors would offer a student a text from the Bible or from another source. The student should then be able to identify its source; quote other texts dealing with the same subject, some leaning to one position and others to the opposite; and then offer and defend the correct alternative.

Thus, Comenius combined an educational theory that was profoundly influenced by rationalism with a theology and theological method that still reflected Protestant scholasticism.

In summary, given the controversies and the enormous political and military challenges of the time, Protestant theologians of the generations after the first reformers devoted their efforts to systematizing the doctrines of those reformers. They did this with a constant insistence on the biblical foundation and on the practical and religious consequences of theology. Although they have been accused of returning to a theology that was very similar to medieval scholasticism the truth is that, at the same time that they made use of Aristotelian logic and of other instruments and methods of that scholasticism, they still remained faithful to the fundamental emphases of the Reformation. Since one of these emphases was human inability before God, this kept them from falling into radical rationalism or giving what they were convinced was too much credit to human reason. At the same time, due to their interest in the "practical" dimensions of theology—that is, its consequences for the life of ethics and devotion—and in the teaching responsibility of ministers, these theologians paid more attention than most of their predecessors to the organization and content of theological studies.

Finally, it is important to point out that, while Protestant scholasticism was radically opposed to Roman Catholicism, it did accept some of its educational views and practices. On matters having to do with theological education, the present chapter may well end with a quote from the 1596 statutes of an Anglican educational institution that shows the influence of the words and even some of the views expressed first by Cardinal Pole and then by the Council of Trent, that theological education was to be understood in term of "seminaries" or seedbeds. According to that document a college should be:

> with regard to the Church, a kind of seminary in which we want only the best seeds to be planted, and these, when planted, watered by abundant showers from the branches of the sciences, until they have grown into the fullness of Christ.[5]

13
The Pietist Reaction

During the eighteenth century a series of movements appeared that may be classified under the common heading of "Pietism." Pietism included the Moravian movement led by Count Zinzendorf, Methodism under the leadership of the Wesley brothers, and in a way also the Great Awakening in North America. It is commonly affirmed—and I myself have said—that Pietism arose as a protest against the intellectualism of Protestant orthodoxy. This is true up to a point. But one must take care not to take it in the sense that the Pietist leaders were anti-intellectuals or that they thought that the education of the ministerial leadership of the church was not important. What concerned them about Protestant scholasticism was not its intellectual rigor but rather that the resulting preaching and pastoral practice did not help the flock to experience the love of Christ more deeply, to grow in faith, and to improve in obedience. Sermons had become long theological disquisitions on points with no clear relevance for the life of the flock. Often the real audience of such sermons was not the congregation present but some other pastor or movement against which the preacher directed his words. Thus, Lutheran orthodox pastors preached against the manner in which the Reformed understood Communion, and the Reformed preached against Lutherans and Arminians, while all Protestants, Lutheran as well as Reformed, preached against Roman Catholicism. There were sermons on the order of the divine decrees—for instance, on whether the decree of predestination is prior to the decree of the fall (supralapsarianism) or follows it (infralapsarianism)—and other similar matters that had little to do with the religious experience of the flock and even less with the nature of obedience in the daily life of business, home, and so forth. As a consequence, for many faith was reduced to attending church—often because the law or society at large demanded it—and obeying a series of ethical precepts that generally coincided with the common morality of society at large.

This was not what the leaders of Protestant scholasticism had proposed in structuring and directing their study programs. Indeed, they all included in such programs devotional practices and character development, while insisting that all theological education must seek to prepare students for ministry within the church. Therefore, their curricula usually included practical disciplines such as homiletics, church management, and leadership of worship. Thus, the radically different theological education that the Pietists sought could not be limited to minor changes in curricula or in educational methods. For this reason, Pietism generally did not focus its attention in the first instance on ministerial training but rather on the nature of faith and of Christian life, in order then to turn to the function of pastors and how they ought to be trained.

Even though similar ideas were circulating widely, Philipp Jakob Spener (1635–1705) is usually credited with the beginning of the movement. Although a Lutheran, Spener had studied in Geneva and tended to look at the differences between Lutherans and Reformed with less acrimony than did the orthodox theologians of either confession. After serving as a professor at the University of Strasbourg, Spener became pastor of a Lutheran church in Frankfort. There, in 1675, he published the most famous of his works, commonly known as *Pia desideria—Pious Desires*, although its complete title was *Pious Desires, or a Sincere Desire for a Reformation of the True Evangelical Church that is Pleasing to God, Jointly with some Simple Christian Answers Addressed to that End*. Furthermore, the first edition of this work was in fact the prologue to a series of sermons by a colleague who shared Spener's ideas. But the impact of *Pia desideria* was such that it was almost immediately published as a separate treatise and soon became one of the most read books in Germany.

After an introduction, Spener's writing is divided into three parts. The first is a lament over the conditions of corruption in which the church is living. Spener mourns the need to point this out, but he is convinced that the church is ill and that the only way to heal an illness is to understand its nature, in order then to seek a remedy and apply it. By corruption Spener does not mean only such obvious matters as sexual improprieties and economic abuses but also the wider issue that much of the true understanding and practice of faith has been lost. The only thing that remains immovable, thanks to God's grace, is divine love as manifested and shared through the word and sacraments. But the truth is that the word is not being preached in such a way that it may reach the hearts of the faithful, and the sacraments have lost much of their meaning for a flock that hardly knows the true nature of faith.

The second part is much more positive. Since Spener trusts the word of God and the sacraments—and behind both the infinite love and inexhaustible grace of God—he also trusts in the future of the church. Thus combining this second part with the first, it is clear that Spener does not doubt the calling of the church or its future but is simply pained that so many in the church do not see that call or live according to that future.

It was the third part of his writing that awakened the most interest. Here Spener proposed six steps leading to the renewal of the church. The first of them was once again to underscore the use and study of scripture, not only as the source of answers to issues being debated but also and above all as a guide for life. This was to be done not only in churches and schools but also in homes, where the study of the Bible should be a fundamental part of family life. Second, Spener proposed a rediscovery of the universal priesthood of believers. Under that heading, he rued the manner in which the clergy had taken possession of the "spiritual priesthood" of all believers—a theme that he had discussed earlier in *Das geistliche Priestertum*. While blaming Roman Catholicism for much of this, he felt that Protestants had allowed themselves to be carried away by the same current. What was then needed was to make clear to all believers that they are priests before God and therefore responsible for all other believers. Third, Spener sought a clear distinction between the knowledge of Christianity and its doctrines on the one hand and the practice of faith on the other. This did not mean that knowledge was unimportant. But it made clear that such knowledge is not the same as lived and experienced faith. This was the foundation for the fourth point, where Spener proposed that, while truth must be defended, this should be done in such a way that controversies would be an example of Christian charity rather than, as was often the case, of bitterness and lack of charity.

The preceding led to the final two points, which related more directly to formal education and ministerial training. The fifth was the need to reform schools and universities so that not only the mind was educated. Today we would say that the purpose of education is not only to inform but also to form.

Without leaving aside the general education of the entire people of God, Spener showed particular preoccupation for the education of those who are to serve as ordained ministers. This was crucial for Spener, since he was convinced that the only way to renew the church was through the teaching and example of its leaders. Candidates for ministry must be exemplary, and they are to be educated in schools and universities whose professors will be guides and mentors taking them by the hand and showing them what they need to know—this, in contrast to those professors whose main goal seems to be to show how much they know.

Finally, in direct connection with the previous point, Spener proposed that sermons should not be opportunities to show the pastor's erudition by means of quotes in foreign languages, nor his mental acuity by detailed and orderly outlines. Nor should they be the occasion to settle controversies over theological minutiae, as if they were addressed to other theologians rather than to the congregation. Rather, preaching should be grounded on the careful study and responsible exegesis of the biblical text and serve for the edification of the body of Christ, appealing not only to the minds of the flock but also to their hearts.

Although much of Spener's fame was due to his *Pia desideria*, what actually most shaped the movement was what he called *ecclesiolae in ecclesia*—smaller churches within the church—and *collegia pietatis*—schools of piety. Although Martin Bucer and others since the time of the Reformation had made similar proposals, the beginning of the *collegia pietatis* dates from a sermon by Spener in 1669 in which he invited those among his flock who wished to do so to gather on Sunday afternoons to learn more about what had been preached in the morning and to cultivate their faith. Soon there were other meetings on Wednesdays, and eventually there were many groups gathering to study scripture, to explore its implications for daily life, and to support one another in faith and in obedience to the gospel. Spener believed that every congregation had a core of believers who wished to live their faith more deeply, and who would then become an *ecclesiola in ecclesia*, not in order to consider themselves better than the rest, but rather to support one another in their quest for a deeper faith.

The success of Pietism was also the result of the interest on the part of Frederick I of Prussia—and after him, of many other rulers from the house of Hohenzollern—in establishing better relationships between their own Calvinism and the Lutheranism of most of their subjects. These rulers saw in Pietism, with its emphasis on the experience of the heart rather than on the details of doctrine, a means for a rapprochement between Lutherans and Calvinists. In 1690 the government of neighboring Saxony dissolved the *collegia pietatis*, and ordered that no scholarships be made available to Pietist candidates for ordination. This led to the exile of both Spener and his most famous follower, August Hermann Francke (1663–1727), to Prussia, whose government welcomed them and established the Pietist University of Halle, which became the main center for the spread of Pietism throughout the world. Furthermore, Frederick I of Prussia banned all preaching against Pietism.

As already stated, the best known of Spener's disciples was Francke. In 1695, thanks to Spener's recommendation, Francke became a professor at Halle, where he spent the rest of his life. He had been influenced by Spener's ideas when, at fourteen years of age, he registered at the University of Erfurt and joined a Bible study group that the students had organized there after the style of the *collegia pietatis* of Spener. There he studied philosophy, theology, rhetoric, and church history, but he soon focused his attention on biblical languages. He then went to University of Leipzig (in Saxony), where he graduated in 1685 and remained as a teacher. In Leipzig he founded the *collegium philobiblicum*—society of friends of the Bible—devoted to the careful study of scripture, combining strict exegesis in the original languages with a more devotional reading of the sacred text. Soon other similar groups began appearing throughout Germany.

The *collegium philobiblicum* became both a complement and a rival to the program of theological study at the University of Leipzig. In the *collegium* Francke gave theological lectures in which he insisted on building everything on a detailed study of scripture and at the same time on relating all to a practical life of devotion and service. These lectures, as well as those delivered by others of similar ideas, became very popular among university students as well as among some pastors and laity. The ensuing rivalry led the theological faculty of the university to forbid their students from attending the lecture at the *collegium philobiblicum*. Eventually, facing such opposition, Francke decided to leave and become a pastor at Erfurt. But many of his students from Leipzig followed him there, so that soon the theological faculty of Erfurt began looking askance at the new pastor and his teaching. Jealousy grew as an ever-increasing number of students showed preference for Francke's lectures over those offered in official courses at the university. And, even worse from the perspective of the university and of the civil authorities, it soon became known that some women were attending the lectures at the *collegium*!

When these and other issues led to difficulties with the government in Saxony and forced him to leave that land, Spener intervened in his favor and had him appointed a pastor in Prussia, as well as an unpaid professor in the recently founded University of Halle, where Francke remained until his death in 1727 and where he made an important contribution to the development of the curricula and organization of the university. He also founded an elementary school for poor children that was supported by donations from his followers, a *seminarium praeceptorium* for the training of elementary school teachers, a *seminarium inselectum* for teachers at the more advanced levels, a boarding school for those preparing to go to university, a shelter for poor students, and a publishing house. Inspired by all of this, Frederick I of Prussia founded several similar schools and programs and decreed that most of the population must have at least a basic education.

At the same time that he was founding and organizing those various institutions, Francke lectured in Halle in a manner similar to what he had done earlier in Leipzig, although now with the support of civil and university authorities, so that soon his methods became general practice of the entire university, eventually making it the most prestigious university in Germany, so that twenty-five years after its foundation it had an enrollment of 1,200 students. There they were expected to work not only on their studies but also in living their faith more profoundly. Most of these students were seeking ordination into the pastoral and missionary ministry—for Halle had become the center of the vast missionary enterprise that may well be credited with the beginning of Protestant missions. As part of their studies, which must be relevant for the actual life of the people, many of the students of theology at the University of Halle were also working as teachers and mentors in the schools that Francke had founded.

The curriculum that these theological students followed was grounded on the study of the Bible in its original languages, with careful exegetical work and always seeking the significance of the text that was being studied for the life of faith, not only of the students themselves but also of the entire community. Therefore, theological education in Halle included a strong emphasis on teaching and pastoral theology not only as separate courses but also as part of the purpose of each course and of the entire program of studies. However, Francke would not allow the practical bent of studies to undercut the academic aspect of the curriculum. Thus, as to the Bible, courses on that subject must include, beside the reading of scripture in its original languages and writing commentaries on every book of the Bible on the basis on that reading, the studies of "auxiliary languages"—that is, languages such as Aramaic and Arabic, which could help to understand the biblical text. Then the curriculum also included courses that dealt more specifically with theology and the history of the church, as well as others that would help the student understand the larger world: studies in languages, geography, history, mathematics, physics, and so forth. All of this was to be done within the context of a strict code of behavior, for the purpose of education was not only to instruct but also to shape character. Such discipline should serve to tame the will and to affirm self-control—in which one hears echoes of medieval monasticism, as well as of the Protestant emphasis on the corruption of the will as a result of sin. But what defines all of this is the matter in which Francke, following Spener, understood the purpose of education, which was to honor God, so that, as Francke himself said in his *Brief and Simple Treatise on Christian Education*, "all good instruction must combine piety with wisdom, leading to a knowledge of Christ through devotion, prayer, study of the Bible, and evangelism."

Another important personality of the history of Pietism is Count Nicholas von Zinzendorf (1700–1760), who guided the Moravians in their formative years. In his early life, Zinzendorf was shaped both by the Pietism of Halle and by the more traditional Lutheranism of Wittenberg. He was never able to study theology, as was his desire, for his family had destined him to civil service and forced him to study law. For this reason as well as others, Zinzendorf's university experience was not pleasant. But, even so, he continued his theological studies on his own account, particularly reading the New Testament in Greek and consulting several of the best biblical scholars of his time. Therefore, although he neither wrote nor said much about theological education in itself, he was concerned that the Moravian leaders that were to become missionaries throughout the world be properly formed at the University of Halle. He saw study as a basic right of every human being. He therefore declared that the educational work of the Moravians should always follow two basic principles. The first was the equality of all before God, regardless of gender, age, or nationality. The second was that the purpose of education is to lead students to an encounter with God and to the life God wants for them.

As to Methodism, one must remember that John Wesley did not intend to create a new church but rather to revitalize the faith of those who already belonged to a church—in most cases, the Church of England. According to his understanding, ordination was basically that of the Church of England, whose pastors were normally educated in the theological schools of the nation—as was Wesley himself, who studied at the University of Oxford. Therefore, Wesley wrote little about ordination and its academic requirements. However, when there were not sufficient ordained ministers to conduct the work of teaching and pastoral care, Wesley was ready to acknowledge and encourage the ministry of lay preachers. Thus, in his journal for April 12, 1789, he says:

> I have uniformly gone for fifty years, never varying from the doctrine of the Church at all; nor from her discipline, of choice, but of necessity: So, in a course of years, necessity was laid upon me, (as I have proved elsewhere): 1. To preach in the open air. 2. To pray extempore. 3. To form societies. 4. To accept the assistance of Lay Preachers.[1]

Thus, while he was not particularly interested in the education of the ordained ministry, he did take great care for the instruction of lay preachers. Therefore, in 1757 he wrote a treatise against errors in religions, which, as he himself said years later in his *Journal* (April 12, 1789), was designed for all those under his care, but particularly for young preachers. For the same reason, he published the *Christian Library*, a collection of fifty books that Wesley thought every preacher must read—even though he himself did not agree with everything said in them. Furthermore, his concern for the education of the people at large was always foremost, as was shown in the school that he founded in Kingswood, which soon became a model imitated by many—at first Methodists and later others from various traditions.

All this is of great importance in order to understand the history of Methodist theological education, particularly in its North American form, which then spread to the rest of the world as a result of the Methodist missionary movement. Although Methodism was born in England, it became an independent church in the United States even before it did in its native land. This North American Methodism had few pastors with the level of education that was expected of Anglican ministers. As the movement moved westward—that is, to the frontier lands taken from their original inhabitants—it became impossible to provide the hundreds of new churches with pastors formed according to the canons of education that the Wesley brothers, Whitefield, and the other founders of Methodism had followed. It was necessary to provide pastoral leadership for new churches in remote places, and this was done by employing lay preachers—a practice that Wesley had already established in England. The educational requirements that applied in England were inadequate for the new situation west of the Atlantic, with the eventual result that the biblical and theological training of many pastors was sorely lacking. In response to that challenge, programs were developed in which pastors could receive and improve their theological education—programs that led to what is known today as the Course of Study. Thus, not all Methodist pastors were formed in seminaries or schools of theology. But at the same time Wesley's original emphasis on theological education, joined to the particular circumstances in the United States, led North American Methodists to undertake a vast educational enterprise not only in biblical and theological matters but in all fields of knowledge. This is the reason why there are now in the United States—and to lesser degree in other parts of the world—hundreds of Methodist colleges and universities, and many others founded by Methodists. It is also for the same reason that, while The United Methodist Church has a dozen seminaries in the United States, still a goodly part of its clergy—particularly those belonging to ethnic minorities or serving in rural areas—do not have formal seminary education.

In summary, there are several important points to be made about Pietism and its impact on ministerial training. First, its emphasis on the need for that training to be practical was not new, for we have already found a similar emphasis among Protestant scholastics as they developed curricula and plans of studies—which shows that the mere assertion that theological education must be practical does not necessarily make it so.

Second, it is important to note that, although they bemoaned the purely intellectual theology of the schools, the leaders of the entire Pietist movement did not oppose education but to the contrary. If they attacked the intellectualism of the scholastics, this was because the latter tended to allow the discussion and acceptance of ideas and doctrines to overshadow the need for feeling and religious experience. But they were convinced that the gospel deserves to be studied and that, just as knowledge is not to be confused with faith, faith is not to be confused with ignorance.

Third, due to its emphasis on the priesthood of all believers, Pietism was concerned for theological education at all levels, although this was to be not a purely rational education but a holistic one, joining what the mind has learned with the feelings of the heart and with the practice of the Christian life. Within the context of universal priesthood, theological education is to be made available to all the faithful, and the particular education that ordained ministers receive is to be directed specifically to their functions as preachers and teachers of the word and administrators of the sacraments.

14
Modern Theological Education

Much of the impact of Pietism on theological education was due to the work of a pastor, theologian, and professor who, while formed in a Pietistic context, also rejected much of Pietism. This was Friedrich Schleiermacher (1768–1834), who was born to a family that had produced several Reformed pastors and chaplains—his father, his two grandfathers, and one of his great-grandfathers. Schleiermacher's father had experienced an awakening in his faith through his contact with the Moravians, and therefore young Schleiermacher was reared in a family of Pietist tendencies and then placed in a Moravian school from which he went to a Moravian seminary. There he read several of the philosophers of the Enlightenment, as well as Spinoza and Kant. Such readings were banned by the seminary, but this did not keep some students from perusing them. Finally, in part due to these readings, Schleiermacher wrote to his father letting him know that he could no longer hold to some elements of Moravian doctrine and that he was therefore leaving the seminary. But even then he did not stop admiring and even retaining some of what he had learned from his Pietist upbringing. Several years later, in a letter, he would say, "After all that has taken place, I have again become a Moravian, only of a higher order."[1] Meanwhile, even amidst his doubts, Schleiermacher passed the required examinations for ordination in the Reformed Church—although he barely passed on dogmatics or doctrinal theology on his second attempt—and began serving as chaplain in a Berlin hospital. There he established contact with Romantic circles—for Romanticism was then in vogue among the German intellectual elites. It was through a combination of his Pietist roots, his Romantic inclinations, and his reading of Kant—which convinced him that religion cannot be founded on reason alone—that Schleiermacher came to the conclusion that the proper seat of religion is neither knowledge nor action—neither doctrine nor morality. The proper seat of religion is "feeling"—*Gefühl.* It was on this basis that he wrote first his *Speeches on Religion*—often simply called Reden—and his great systematic theology *Glaubenslehre*—translated into English as *The Christian Faith.*

However, what is of most interest for our present subject is his *Brief Outline of Theological Studies*, which he wrote in 1811, soon after being appointed as a professor in the recently founded University of Berlin. (Schleiermacher himself had been one of three members of the committee that wrote the bylaws for the university in 1810.) It was in that context that he proposed a curriculum in which theology would be studied under three headings: philosophical theology, dogmatic theology, and pastoral theology. The first would seek to determine what Christianity is as a particular form of the feeling of dependence on God and its place amid the context of other religious feelings. For this reason, Schleiermacher is often credited with having made room in the theological curriculum for philosophy of religion and through it to comparative religions. This philosophical theology is not to be based on the "natural theology" of Deism, which proved untenable after the critiques of Hume and Kant, but on the "feeling of absolute dependence" that is at the very root of all religious experience and takes a particular form in the Christian faith.

The second field of studies, historical theology, would be dedicated to the life and teachings of the church through the ages, as well as to the study of that life and those teachings in the present. In this second theological field dogmatics must have an important place. What is understood here by "dogmatics" is the study of the teachings of the church at a given moment and particularly in the present. His interest was not in relating dogma to philosophy—which is the reason why Schleiermacher insisted on placing dogma under the heading of historical theology rather than under systematic theology. Nor is he interested in grounding dogma on philosophical considerations but rather on its relation to the feeling of absolute dependency on God as the church lives it at a particular time thanks to its relationship with Jesus Christ. Thus, Schleiermacher's theology is radically christocentric. Since the purpose of this theology is to serve the church as a concrete community of faith, dogmatics must be deeply rooted in that community, not only in general or universal terms but also in the concrete way in which that community exists in a given time and place—that is, the church here and now. This does not make historical theology and dogmatics inferior to philosophy, for the feeling of dependence on God always takes place within a community—in the case of Christianity, of the church in its relation with Jesus Christ.

In summary, historical theology is much more than what that title now implies. It includes first of all biblical studies, which deal with the historical origins and the first expressions of the Christian faith. Then, it includes the entire process leading from biblical times to the present—that is, what today we call "history of Christianity" and "history of theology." And finally it includes the Christian faith in its present expression as the concrete and specific way in which a community of faith lives and experiences the feeling of absolute dependence on God as it has been bequeathed to it by the entire process, from biblical times to the present. Such studies are absolutely necessary in order to understand the place of the present church as a concrete expression of the feeling of absolute dependence. All of this is an indication of the degree to which critical and historical studies dominated the intellectual scene early in the nineteenth century. Instead of rejecting such studies, as was done by the more conservative—including much of the traditional pietism he had rejected in his youth—or allowing himself to be carried away by such studies as if the essence of faith were to be found in them, Schleiermacher did value them, not as leading to an understanding of what Christianity is in its essence but rather as a way to understand how the life of the church, expressing its feeling of absolute dependency on God, has developed to the present, and how in consequence of this the present church lives and expresses that feeling.

Finally, practical theology focuses on all that is necessary to function as a leader within the community of faith. For this reason, Schleiermacher has been called the "father of practical theology," even though what he understood by that term was not the entire gamut of disciplines that today are included under that heading, but rather a manner of doing theology that would take into account the feeling of absolute dependence as it is expressed in the specific community in which one is to serve and also takes into account how that feeling is to be nourished and expressed.

In order to understand the manner in which Schleiermacher viewed and defended theological studies at the university, one must realize that this was the time of the Enlightenment, which was accompanied by the growth of scientific methodology and which therefore tended to exclude theological and religious studies from the university. In the modern university, for which the one in Berlin was intended to be a model, science would rule, and fields such as theology would have to justify their presence. Ironically, theology, which centuries earlier had given birth to the universities, now had to defend its place within them. In order to do so, Schleiermacher and others like him had to show that theology is a science—a *Wissenschaft*, which may be translated as "science" although not necessarily in the sense of following the methodology of empirical disciplines, but rather in the sense of having a specific and critical methodology. This is true of each of the three elements of theological studies, which Schleiermacher calls "philosophical theology," "historical theology," and "practical theology."

The diversity of opinions in the nineteenth and twentieth centuries produced an enormous variety of philosophical theologies. Among these, the philosophy of Schleiermacher's contemporary G. W. F. Hegel soon dominated Western thought. Applying Hegelianism, theological systems emerged that claimed that Christianity was a culmination of the dialectic of the Spirit, as Hegel understood it. From that time, and well into the twenty-first century, countless theologians sought to justify their presence in the academic world either by linking their theology to a particular philosophical stance or by reducing it to historical and critical inquiry and thus claiming for it the objectivity that science claimed for itself.

In what Schleiermacher had called "historical theology," the historical critical method undercut much of what earlier had been taken for granted both in church history and in biblical studies. Historians and biblical scholars had to show that their studies were scientific, and therefore the purpose of these studies was no longer to inquire as to what the history of the church or the Bible meant for the life of society and of the church, but rather to attain a "scientific" knowledge of the Bible as well as of history.

This produced both great benefits and great losses. As to its benefits, there is no doubt that the historical critical method led to a clearer understanding of the origins of biblical texts as well as of the practices and doctrines of the church. Without such knowledge, we would not know where to place the last chapters of Isaiah in their historical context, nor could we determine the chronological order of the epistles of Paul, nor the relationship among the various gospels. The loss was in that, although the texts and the formative movements in the life of the church were better understood, it became increasingly difficult to know what to do with them in the life of the church. For instance, New Testament studies offered cogent solutions to what came to be called the "synoptic problem," and to this day the result helps us understand the parallelisms and the differences among the first three Gospels. But those studies themselves had little to say about the authority of the Gospels or their relevance for the life of the church and of believers. Thus, in biblical as well as in historical studies, emphasis was made on objectivity. The true biblical scholar or the true historian worthy of being part of a university faculty must be able to study the Bible or the history of the church with the same objectivity with which an entomologist studies an insect under a microscope. In all of this one may see the impact of modernity, with its emphasis on objective, verifiable, and universal knowledge—and it is not by chance that some of the theological tendencies resulting from this trend came to be called "modernism."

In the field of practical theology, this led into two directions. On the one hand, such studies became increasingly excluded from theological schools, for they were practical rather than critical and therefore unworthy of the scientific environment of the university. Thus, when in 1958 I went to study in Strasbourg, I was surprised to learn that students in the theology faculty at that university would spend four years studying Bible, history, and theology, and that it was only after having been examined in those fields that they went to the *Stiftung*, where they would learn how to preach, lead worship, serve as pastors, and so forth. On the other hand, and in the opposite direction, there were cases in which, in order to justify their presence in the university, teachers of such practical disciplines became obsessed with objectivity to the level that bordered on the ridiculous. Thus, some time ago I met a professor of homiletics whose claim to fame was that he had developed a "scientific" method to prepare and evaluate sermons by means of a complicated mathematical formula based on counting certain words and seeking or applying geometric principles to the construction of the sermon!

Something similar, although not to such an extreme, took place both in Great Britain and in the United States. Institutions such as Harvard and Yale had begun as schools of theology—actually, as small programs in which a pastor would periodically meet with a group of candidates in order to give them instruction and mentoring. In the nineteenth century the impact of the European model, after the style of the University of Berlin, was such that it led these and other universities in directions in which faculties of theology found themselves in constant danger of being marginalized. In response to that danger, many sought to justify their presence by means of an insistence on their own objectivity and their use of the historical critical method.

In the midst of all this, the explosion in scientific knowledge, joined with results of the historical critical study of scripture, has had three important consequences. The first of these was the conflict between fundamentalists and liberals. While liberalism and modernism may be seen as the result of the surrender of theologians before modernity, fundamentalism was also a less obvious surrender, for it was as modern as liberalism in its quest for objective and universal truths. The difference was mostly that, while liberalism sought those truths in one place, fundamentalism sought them in another. Among some liberals, the Bible came to be little more than a document about the primitive beliefs of Israel and the ancient church. Its value, besides providing information about those ancient beliefs, was in its literary beauty or in the wisdom of some of its advice. For fundamentalists, any modern discovery was to be rejected if it did not agree with the literal, supposedly objective and universal reading of the Bible as if it were a book of science. In some cases in which modern knowledge was irrefutable it was accepted, but then one sought a means to show that the Bible did not contradict it. An example is the matter of how Joshua stopped the sun, when today we know that the sequence of day and night is not due to the movement of the sun, but rather of the earth. But except in those few cases, fundamentalists tended to reject many of the discoveries and theories that seemed to contradict the teaching of scripture. One could then say that the result was the "canonization of ignorance," in which theologians and religious leaders insisted on their traditional positions, ignoring the challenges of modernity. A remarkable example is the famous theologian Charles Hodge (1797–1878) of whom it is said that when leaving his teaching position at Princeton Theological Seminary after a long tenure, he declared himself proud that during all of those years, he had not allowed a single new idea to enter the seminary!

The impact of such conditions varied from church to church and from country to country, but it was felt for long years. In the United States, schools such as Harvard and Yale (the first founded in 1636 and the second in 1701) became centers of research modeled after the University of Berlin. The College of New Jersey—today Princeton University—supported the creation of a school of theology, but when this was founded in 1812 by action of the General Assembly of the Presbyterian Church, it was created as an independent institution. The history of that institution and of its rivals is the history of the theological debates that took place during the nineteenth century and early in the twentieth. During a good part of the nineteenth century, that seminary was known for its defense of a traditional and orthodox Calvinism, particularly under the leadership of the above-mentioned Reformed theologian Charles Hodge (1797–1878). Already in 1836, Presbyterians and others of liberal inclinations felt that Princeton was too conservative, and therefore founded what is now Union Theological Seminary in New York City. The controversy was prolonged. In 1929, under the leadership of John Gresham Machen (1881–1937), several professors complained that liberalism had become dominant in Princeton, left that seminary, and founded Westminster Theological Seminary near the city of Philadelphia. In 1936—a hundred years after the founding of Union—as it became clear that the Presbyterian Church would continue supporting Princeton, that group abandoned the church and created the Orthodox Presbyterian Church.

Second, the development of the sciences in the nineteenth and twentieth centuries complicated the theological curriculum through a huge expansion in the field of "practical theology." What in the time of Schleiermacher was mostly a theological discipline, devoted to critical reflection on the practice of ministry, now turned into a series of disciplines mostly independent among themselves, and each built on the discoveries and theories of a new secular discipline. Thus, psychology, which came into vogue after discoveries of Sigmund Freud (1856–1939), Alfred Adler (1870–1937), Carl Jung (1875–1961), Erich Fromm (1910–80), and others, gave birth to pastoral psychology, sometimes called pastoral counseling, in which one sought to employ the new psychological knowledge and theories in pastoral practice. Something similar took place in the field of education, where the theories of John Dewey (1859–1952) and others became the norm for the early stages of a new discipline called "Christian education." Later, new theories and practices in the field of communications made an impact on homiletics. Something similar may also be said about sociology, economics, and the more recent theories and practices in business management. Frequently, there was a closer connection between those disciplines and their secular counterparts than between them and the theological curriculum at large. For instance, a biblical and theological critique of counseling practices and theories born out of the secular practice and theory of counseling and therapy was seldom attempted. Likewise, there were courses on church management that simply took the latest theories on business management and applied them to management in the church, with little consideration of their theological implications. It is also interesting to know that, partly because of that lack of theological reflection, the new disciplines of "practical theology" were able to overcome some of the theological debates between liberals and fundamentalists.

And third, the explosion of knowledge in the nineteenth and twentieth centuries led to a process of ever-greater specialization. Until shortly before that time, it had been possible to be well versed in most of the existing knowledge. Thus, the great figures of the Renaissance could aspire to what they called *l'uomo universale*—the universal human being—which meant being able to delve into all the fields of knowledge and human activity. In some of the curricula that developed earlier, it was expected that the candidate for ministry would not only know Bible and theology but also classical literature, history, astronomy, and even medicine. But now the explosion of knowledge made such goals unattainable and led to specialization. While in antiquity, and until fairly recently, an educated person was able to be up to date on several themes and disciplines, in modernity this became impossible. Growing specialization meant that those who studied zoology knew little of botany and nothing of astronomy. Soon among the zoologists some became entomologists, others herpetologists, and so forth. And the entomologists knew little about snakes, while the herpetologists knew little about insects.

In the field of ministerial studies and pastoral practice, this has four important consequences. One of them is that the ordained ministry no longer has the privileged position it had before, when in any town or village the pastor was the most highly educated person, and therefore the one to whom all went in search of guidance and counsel not only in religious matters but also in many others. Today, due to the process of specialization, there are no universal experts. Today the pastor is often seen as a specialist in matters of Bible and religion, but as only one among many whom one consults according to different needs—the physician in times of illness, the lawyer in times of litigation, the architect for construction, and so forth.

The second consequence, partly resulting from the first, was the already mentioned "canonization of ignorance." Since today the cardiologist can declare with impunity not to know the first word about geography or physics, so can today's minister declare not to know about other things than Bible and religion. But there is a great difference that must be pointed out. In the first place, the cardiologist who declares ignorance on matters of geography or physics did study physics and geography before reaching the school of medicine. In such specialization one is not totally ignorant on matters of general knowledge. On the contrary, the cardiologist who confesses not to know physics does so because she has studied sufficient physics to have an idea of how much more there is to be known. And, precisely because of this awareness of how much remains unknown, a cardiologist does not attempt to apply her medical knowledge in the field of physics or geography but is willing to acknowledge the value of those other studies, while acknowledging her lack of knowledge in them. In contrast, a pastor who takes refuge in a supposed specialization in Bible and theology in order to hide what he or she does not know has simply canonized ignorance. Such "canonization of ignorance" leads to what could well be called "biblical imperialism," in which the pastor, on no other grounds than being a supposed specialist on divine matters, attempts to tell scientists how to follow their disciplines. As a consequence, the message of the gospel is isolated and is interpreted in such a way that it has little to say to those who do not accept such biblical imperialism. This is why, while there are groups in which people educated in different fields gather in order to share some of their knowledge, experience, and ideas, there are pastors who purposely stay away from such circles. Their biblical imperialism is simply another face of their canonized ignorance, which isolates them from those who do not accept the pastor's imperialism but do see the pastor's ignorance.

The third consequence of the process of specialization in various disciplines is particularly seen in European and American schools with abundant resources. This is the specialization within the very field of theological and pastoral studies. The model that appeared in most of the better seminaries—that is, those that did not follow the path of canonizing ignorance—was one of specialization both in teaching and in ministry. Given all that is known today about the Bible, its languages, its origins, its transmission, and so forth, and all that is known about history, psychology, and communications, any one of those fields provides more than enough material to keep a professor fully occupied. Thus it would seem that the more specialists an institution has the better its teaching will be. We need a professor of pastoral counseling, and the main requirement for that position is to be adept in psychology, while knowing little or nothing about Bible, theology, history, or education is not an impediment. As long as one is a true specialist in a particular subject, that suffices. The counterpart of this is the specialization of the students themselves. Thus, one knows Bible, but not preaching, and the other is proficient in education but knows little theology; while one prepares to practice pastoral counseling, one should not be asked to preach. Thus it happens that it is precisely in the supposedly better schools, where there is an abundance of specialists, that students have most difficulty integrating their studies.

The majority of theological schools and seminaries in the former mission fields do not have the size or the resources necessary for such a degree of specialization. It is significant, however, that many of these institutions see this as a deficiency that must be corrected. Perhaps it would be best if they saw in this an opportunity to reflect on what could be the best theological education in their own context.

As a result of all this, the fourth consequence of the process of specialization is the compartmentalization of the theological curriculum. Instead of a process of formation of the whole person, the theological curriculum becomes a series of courses, much as a series of requirements to fulfill, and the formation of the candidate for ministry as a whole person moves to the background. Once again, although this happened first and foremost in European and North American schools, soon other seminaries in lands that have received missionaries from those areas followed the same model, also coming to conceive of the curriculum as a series of relatively independent courses and paying ever less attention to the formation of their candidates as whole persons.

This also has had an impact on the literature being produced. Following the example of universities, theological faculties and seminaries came to think that an important and even indispensable measure of the value of the professor is research and publication—hence the well-known principle of "publish or perish." A large portion of books and other material published today on biblical and theological subjects have little usefulness for ministerial training or practice or for the life of the church at large. One of the reasons is that much of such literature has been a response, not to the needs of the church or to the society in general, but rather to the need of their authors to publish something that will advance their academic careers. Since generally such publications are not judged on the basis of their relevance but their originality and precision, the result is a vast number of books written to make an impression on colleagues in whose hands lies the author's future.

Most of the above is true both of Roman Catholic theological education as well as of its Protestant counterpart. The principles established by the Council of Trent in the sixteenth century ruled the training of priests until well into the twentieth. The decision of Trent to create "seminaries" for the instruction and

113

formation of priests had as a consequence a highly educated clergy, well prepared for constant polemics against Protestantism—particularly since Protestantism also had highly educated ministers formed in Protestant universities and schools of theology. The foremost figure in the application of the decrees of Trent was Saint Vincent de Paul (1581–1660), who founded several seminaries and emphasized the need for such institutions to encourage not only knowledge but also development and spiritual formation.

When the Second Vatican Council gathered, the formation of the clergy was not part of its initial agenda. But as the deliberations moved forward, it became necessary to deal with the matter, and therefore in 1965, almost at the end of its sessions, the council issued two decrees, *Optatam totius* and *Presbyteriorum ordinis*. In these two decrees the council set some general principles, directing that each regional conference of bishops should decide what the specific curriculum should be for its region and that such proposals would be submitted to the Holy See for its approval. Without contradicting the decisions of Trent, that seminaries are seedbeds necessary for the formation of young men training for priesthood, the Second Vatican Council declared that students in such institutions should be in contact with the realities of society at large and particularly with their own families. As to the curriculum itself, the first principle to be followed is that "students receive careful training on the sacred Scripture, which is to be the soul of theology." On this basis the council decreed that

> the following order should be observed in the treatment of dogmatic theology: biblical themes should have first place; then students should be shown what the Fathers of the Church, both of the East and of the West, have contributed toward the faithful transmission and elucidation of each of the revealed truths; then the later history of dogma, including its relation to the general history of the Church; lastly, in order to throw as full a light as possible on the mysteries of salvation, the students should learn to examine more deeply, with the help of speculation and with St. Thomas as teacher, all aspects of these mysteries and to perceive their interconnection.[2]

Furthermore, since clergymen have to be teachers, priests, and pastors, their training has to be directed to those functions. As prospective teachers, students must study and learn how to proclaim the word of God. As future priests, they must know how to direct worship and how such worship relates to the process of sanctification. And as pastors in formation, they must know how to lead the faithful and how to serve others.

In all of this, the actions of the Second Vatican Council, while reinforcing what had been done in Trent, tended to underscore the central role of scripture and the connection between the ordained priesthood and the priesthood of all believers—a connection that the council never defined.

In summary, partly due to Schleiermacher's impact and also as a result of a series of circumstances already reflected in Schleiermacher's work, modern theological education was born out of a combination of Pietist goals with the new scientific and critical mentality. Soon, both in European universities and in most North American universities and seminaries, the critical and scientific tended to eclipse the Pietistic impulse so that it became clear that the main criterion determining which were the best schools was not so much their relevance for the church and for its ministry as the prestige of the school itself and its teachers among their colleagues at the universities and other seminaries. Such judgment was based on the originality and thoroughness of the research conducted by the faculty, particularly as reflected in its publications, rather than on the impact that the graduates of such institutions might make on the church and on society.

The emphasis on critical studies, particularly regarding the Bible, was one of the elements leading to the conflict between fundamentalists and liberals, in which they first rejected critical studies, and the latter gave them an absolute and final value. Thus, while the former canonized ignorance and promoted a sort of biblical imperialism, some among the latter canonized science and promoted studies and discussions that had little relevance for the life of the church and for its pastors.

This led to increasing tension between the academy and the church. For a time, several traditional denominations opted for fundamentalism, breaking fellowship with those who disagreed and condemning every position that did not agree with every detail of what the church had declared to be biblical truth. In return, there was among university institutions—including those created and supported by churches—a tendency to grow apart from the church.

As this was taking place in Europe and the North Atlantic, most Protestant churches in the rest of the world were still subject to their mother churches— many structurally and financially, and most in their view of mission. Even unwittingly, most of these younger churches sought to imitate their mother churches, and this was also the case in the field of theological education. For this reason, seminaries throughout the world became—and many still are—reflections of institutions of theological education in their mother churches. While the lack of resources has usually impeded extreme specialization and the application of the "publish or perish" principle, there are still many in the younger churches that see this as a deficiency.

15
A Brief Overview

As we review what we have learned, the first point to be noted is that seminaries are a relatively recent invention. They date from the sixteenth century, when they were first established by the Roman Catholic Church. Before that time there were no seminaries. There were indeed universities in which theology was studied. But the purpose of such studies was not to train for pastoral ministry but rather to gain a deeper understanding of the faith and in some cases to combat doctrines considered heretical. This means that no matter how much we value these institutions that are called seminaries or schools of theology and no matter how important the role they play in the church today, they are not part of the essence of the church. The church can exist, and indeed did exist for fifteen centuries, without seminaries. Furthermore, it was only in the time of the Reformation, when seminaries were beginning to be founded, that churches, Catholic as well as Protestant, began to require specific studies for ordination.

But at the same time it is necessary to remember that in its better times the church has always had a highly educated pastoral ministry and that one of the characteristics of the lesser times has been an ignorant clergy. In the ancient church, it was common and almost expected that those elected as bishops or pastors had a certain degree of education. At a time when there was a high degree of illiteracy, it was expected that the bishop or pastor at least know how to read, even in the small and remote communities. Most of the great leaders of the ancient church were highly educated persons. Usually, they had studied rhetoric, which at that time was the main subject of schools, and their commitment to the gospel led them to seek to learn more about faith and scripture—sometimes, as was the case with Saint Augustine, quite apart from any desire to be ordained; in other cases, as with Saint Ambrose, it took place after ordination, in order better to fulfill the various ministerial tasks.

Combining these two elements—on the one hand the lack of schools and of educational requirements, and on the other, the importance of education and theology—the ancient church expected that once elected to the episcopacy, one would send a theological statement to nearby prospective colleagues, who in turn would express their approval by participating in the ordination of the new bishop. Thus, although formal theological studies were never required for ordination, it was expected that those to be ordained have at least a basic knowledge of theology and scripture.

But there is another element that is often forgotten and should also lead to some serious reflections regarding the relation between studies and ordination. For most of us, theological studies are a preparation for the ordained ministry, much as medical studies are a preparation for the practice of medicine. For this reason, many of our discussions regarding theological education have to do with the academic requirements for ordination, how to help pastors be more effective, and so forth. All of this may be very important, but it is grounded on a misunderstanding as to the main reason why theology is to be studied. Theological studies are not the specialty of the ordained ministry, like medical studies are the specialty of physicians, but rather the way in which the church and all its members, both jointly and individually, express our love for God, as the commandment says, with all our minds. When believers study scripture, we do not do this because it is an ordination requirement, but because in it we find the word of God for our lives and for the life of the church. One should study theology, not in order to pass an examination but in order to learn how to see everything—including the life of the church—in the light of the word and action of God. Whoever studies the history of the church should do so not because it is required, but because this history is part of our inheritance—much like the stories of our families that we learned on our grandmothers' laps. This is what we have seen in our overview in cases such as that of Augustine, who did not study theology in order to be ordained but simply because his own faith led him to it. This is what we hear in the words of Anselm: "no matter how imperfectly, I wish to understand your truth, that truth that my heart believes and loves."[1] That is what we see throughout the ancient church, in which the main form of theological education was the catechumenate—an education that some continued because their faith led them to do so, with the result that some among them were then elected pastors. It is because we have forgotten this that we have developed an entire system of theological education quite apart from Christian education, with the inevitable result that the laity comes to think of biblical and theological studies as a matter for specialists. Thus is lost the fundamental dimension of biblical and theological studies as part of the life of the entire people of God and as expression of loving God with all our minds.

The remedy for this must be no less than a radical transformation in theological education—a transformation that cannot be limited to curricular matters or to means of communication and evaluation but must be grounded on a renewed vision of theological education. In this vision, all of Christian life is, among other things, a life of theological study and reflection. This should lead to an uninterrupted continuity between Christian education as it is provided in the local church and that which is available to more advanced students. Every believer—not only those who seek ordination—is called to learn as much as possible about the Bible, theology, the history of the church, and the practice of faith in today's world.

Returning to our bird's eye view, there are two other elements that must be underscored regarding ministerial training during the first centuries of the life of the church. The first is the important role of pastoral and theological mentors. Once forced to accept ordination, Ambrose sent for Simplician to be his theological mentor. There are many similar cases that could be mentioned. Second, as one reviews the matter in the ancient church, and particularly as we move into the Middle Ages, one is impressed by the existence of a number of writings whose purpose was the instruction of the clergy. Among them one could mention Ambrose's *On the Duties of the Clergy*, Gregory's *Pastoral Rule*, and the *Institutions* of Cassiodorus. Likewise, after the invention of the printing press, Melanchthon's *Loci Theologici* and Calvin's *Institutes* came to be required reading, the former among Lutherans and the latter among the Reformed. John Wesley compiled and published his *Christian Library*, which included fifty books that he invited every believer—and certainly all Methodist preachers—to read and to study. The personal contact of mentors and preachers on the one hand and the less personal but more generalized contact with valuable books on the other have always been part of the task of theological education and still continue to be so.

As a further point in our survey, one may note that when Christian schools began developing during the Middle Ages, these were first monastic schools, then cathedral schools, and finally universities. Although the main purpose of these schools was not the training of people for the clergy, they did produce some of the most outstanding pastors in the Middle Ages. When at the time of the Reformation the Council of Trent decreed the founding of "seminaries" for the training of clergy, this was understood in terms of communities of study and character formation that would be very similar to the earlier monastic communities. Soon Protestantism began to follow a similar pattern, particularly in the United States and Great Britain, and Protestant seminaries came to be study centers in which community life was part of clerical formation. This is the reason why to this day many Protestant seminaries both in Europe and in the United States—and in churches resulting from North Atlantic missions—stress life in community.

The Reformation and the many polemics that it produced led to greater emphasis on the academic training of ministers, Catholic as well as Protestant. This is particularly true beginning in the seventeenth century, when Protestant scholasticism and Catholic anti-Protestant polemics required that pastors have a solid theological education. The result was that most churches established academic requirements that candidates must have met before being ordained, and in most of the denominations that did not have such a requirement, it was expected that those who were able to study would do so.

Eighteenth-century Pietism, exemplified in the University of Halle and in the Methodism of the Wesley brothers, while holding orthodox theological views, insisted on the need of a theology and a preaching addressed more directly to the heart and not only to the mind. As part of these movements, the University of Halle became a center for the training of missionaries, and Methodism established quite a few schools not only for the general education of the public but also for the training of its preachers.

The nineteenth century, with its emphasis on the sciences and critical and objective thought, resulted in the founding of new universities such as the one in Berlin and in the reformation of other universities, so that all disciplines were to be subjected to the requirement of critical objectivity. In the field of theology, this led to theological studies that were more critical and rational, but also more distanced from the needs of preachers and pulpits.

In this entire process theological education in what had earlier been called mission fields—that is, in the "younger churches"—tended to follow the patterns of the mother churches and of theological education in the lands from whence the missionaries came. Therefore, the vision of a seminary that long ruled in those younger churches was that of an institution similar to the North American and British schools where many missionaries had been formed and which now also trained people from the younger churches who went to study in them in order to return to their native lands and there devote themselves to theological education.

Today a series of factors lead to questioning those patterns. Some have been mentioned before, and some are relatively new so that it is difficult to foretell their consequences. Among those factors mentioned earlier, the first to be taken into account is the expansion of knowledge and its ensuing specialization. With each day that passes, what a particular human being is able to know becomes an ever-diminishing fraction of the totality of human knowledge. No matter how much pastors know, and no matter how much they have studied, there will always be in their congregations people who in their own fields have more knowledge and expertise than the pastor. Furthermore, even in theological studies themselves, there has been an explosion of knowledge such that not even by devoting one's entire life to studying, for instance, the Gospel of Matthew, is it possible to know all that is known, is discussed, and has been discovered about that particular book.

This leaves two alternatives that have already been mentioned but that must be underscored. The first alternative is to tell students that they will be specialists in Bible and theology and therefore will not have to know much about other subjects. This is what I have called the canonization of ignorance. On the basis of such positions, pastors may feel secure. Their task is only to affirm and reaffirm what the Bible says and what their theological tradition—Catholic, Lutheran, Reformed, or Pentecostal—tells them to teach. From the pinnacle of their biblical and theological knowledge, such pastors can speak authoritatively on any cultural issue—no matter whether it has to do with biology, psychology, economics, or any other subject. No matter what the issue may be, pastors do not have to know anything about the subject being discussed, for the authority of the Bible is used for canonizing ignorance. The pastor then approaches any subject under discussion much as the Spanish conquistadores did when they arrived at the Western hemisphere: convinced that, because they had the truth, they did not have to listen to the wisdom of others. This immediately leads to "biblical imperialism": the Bible becomes an instrument of control, just as earlier it was an instrument of conquest and colonization.

The other alternative is much more difficult. In this other case, what ministerial education is to seek is not only that candidates for orders know the Bible and theology but above all that they know how to employ that knowledge in such a way as to encourage dialogue with the rest of human knowledge. This is more demanding than the previous alternative for at least two reasons. The first is that frequently all that the churches want is people who know and support their doctrines and who have the necessary abilities to take care of a congregation. The second is simply that it is much easier to teach people what they ought to think than to teach them to think. But no matter how difficult this may be, it is absolutely necessary. No seminary professor or ecclesiastical leader knows what will be the new circumstances that the church and its members will face in the near future. If we are to prepare leaders for a future that we cannot fully envision, it does not suffice to teach them how to think and what to do. They also have to be trained in such a way that they will know how to respond to unexpected circumstances and challenges on the basis of solid theological and biblical principles. If we don't prepare such leaders, when those circumstances and challenges arrive the church will not know how to respond to them, and in consequence it will seem irrelevant and will be increasingly marginalized.

No matter how good the teaching and training in our seminaries and other theological education institutions, no teaching and training will be sufficient for those who are graduating today and will be serving as pastors until the middle of the century. This implies that theological education cannot end with a certificate, diploma, or degree. Such documents, frequently seen as declarations that studies have been completed, in reality can be no more than a certification that one is ready to serve in the present moment and to continue studying.

Another theme that appeared frequently in our historical review is that of a community of study and formation. In the letters of Cyprian, in the third century, there are references to the training of new leaders, apparently in community with those who had already attained such positions. Certainly, in the community founded by Saint Augustine, which eventually became the model for the Augustinian Canons, we find the same emphasis on study and devotion based on a life in common. The same emphasis appears in the medieval monastic and cathedral schools and, to a certain degree, in the early universities, which were in truth conglomerations of houses or communities of study—for instance, those of the Dominicans and the Franciscans in Paris, Oxford, and Salamanca. In some modern universities, dominated as they are by competence and individual achievement, much of that community spirit is lost. But even so, some of those ancient universities continue the old tradition of having "colleges" where community life is the context for study.

Modern seminaries retain that emphasis, for the traditional view of a seminary is a residential community where students and their families live together, worship jointly with frequency and regularity, share at least some meals, have joint recreational programs, and so forth. In all of this, the common view of a seminary reflects the legacy of the older monastic schools, where all lived in community, had fixed and regular times of prayer, ate together, and had fixed periods for common recreation.

This model of ministerial education in the context of such community has its values and its dangers. The most obvious among its values is that it facilitates the process of developing discipline and character. In such circumstances the entire community—students as well as faculty—becomes an opportunity to develop disciplines of study and devotion, and to practice and develop habits and ways of relating to others and responding to them. There is no doubt that such disciplines and habits are necessary for the practice of ministry. On the other hand, the very word *seminary* points to the main danger in this model of theological education. In its initial use, a seminary was a seedbed. In a garden, the main purpose of a seedbed is to keep young plants in a protective environment in which it is easier to control weeds and insects, in order then to transplant them to the place where they are to grow. It was thus that the seminaries proposed by the Council of

Trent were conceived. And it is thus that some of today's residential seminaries function—or at least are expected to function. This is the vision of those church leaders who insist that seminaries should keep their students from all "contamination" of extraneous ideas. The problem is that in transplanting the candidate from such a seedbed to the actual life in the rest of society, often that very formation in the seedbed makes it difficult to return to the wider community in which ministry is to take place.

In recent times, the model of theological education in a residential community—which could be called a semimonastic model—has become ever more difficult and even unsustainable. This is due to several well known reasons: while in earlier times almost all students were single males, now many have families, and this in itself hinders the semimonastic model. Furthermore, churches do not have the necessary resources—or do not wish to invest those they do have—to support such semimonastic communities, particularly in view of the greater economic needs of students with families. Many students have to earn their living by working outside the seminary, and therefore they can only be part-time students. Within families, the studies of the children and the work of students' spouses make it more difficult to move in order to live in the seminary. For these reasons and several others, the residential model patterned after the medieval monastic schools is becoming less prevalent, as students take their courses in the evenings and weekends, in extension programs, or through the Internet.

In comparing these new developments with the older residential model, we see that they, too, have their values and their dangers. Their main value is that, in contrast with what happens in a seminary/seedbed, students remain actively engaged in the context in which they are to serve as pastors. This is true not only of their lives in society but also of their lives within the church, which normally then take place in the context of an actual congregation and not—as sometime happens in seminaries—within the context of a community that always has a certain degree of artificiality. In other words, this model avoids the difficulties of having to transplant the students back to the society and the church in which ministry will take place. On the other hand, these new models risk the danger of underestimating the importance of theological education as formation—formation of discipline, of habits, and of character. In these new models, it is easy to imagine that ministerial training consists in a series of courses that the candidate must complete. In that case, ministerial training tends to become a matter of instruction and not of formation. It is relatively easy to instruct another person by distance learning, be it by correspondence, as became relatively common in the latter half of the twentieth century, or through cyberspace, as is done today.

Since the Internet has been mentioned, it is important that leaders of theological education reflect about what this new means of communication and information implies for the task of theological education. As a beginning for such reflection, it may be useful to suggest that what is happening in our time is parallel to what took place in the sixteenth century, when the invention of the printing press multiplied the number of books and their accessibility to an ever wider public. Martin Luther was one of the first to make use of the printing press for the diffusion of his ideas, and through that diffusion to undermine the power of traditional authorities that tried to suppress his ideas. The impact of John Calvin through his *Institutes of the Christian Religion* was much greater than his impact as a reformer in Geneva. Thanks to the printing press, a growing number of books began circulating proposing all sorts of doctrines. Therefore, one of the greater issues that churches had to face was how to make certain that the great variety of books and doctrines would not mislead the people and even their pastors. The response of the Roman Catholic Church to this challenge was the *Index of Forbidden Books*, which was first published in 1559, and repeatedly updated as new books appeared whose doctrines or opinions the church rejected—until 1948, when the last such revision was made. Obviously, this did not have the desired result, for it was impossible to keep up to date with the growing number of books published throughout the world and the teachings they contained. Also, as usually happens in such cases, the very prohibition of a book awakened curiosity, and therefore the *Index* led many to read various materials precisely because they were forbidden. Although some Protestants followed a parallel course, most opted for a more difficult but eventually more effective alternative. Rather than forbidding the reading of books that contradicted the teachings of the church, what they sought was to enable the leaders of the church, and in so far as possible the entire church, to judge wisely as to the value of any book and the truth or error of what was said in it. The first of these options was more consistent with the view of theological education as taking place in a seminary or seedbed, whose purpose is to keep students away from the contagion of false doctrines. The second enabled them to recognize and combat such doctrines.

The Internet is having a similar but much deeper impact. One may search for any subject and find solid studies and discussions, but one will also find many baseless and uninformed claims and opinions. One may look up, for instance, "Jezebel," and learn the meaning of her name, her place within the history of Israel, and much more. But one would also learn that any church that does not belong to a particular "apostolic network" is actually the "church of Jezebel." In the Internet one may find some excellent studies on Calvin's eschatology, but one could also find someone who declares that in exactly three years, two months, four days, and five hours the Lord will return. One may find profound christological meditations, and one will also find a character who claims that he is both Jesus Christ and the Beast. And the greatest difficulty is not with such ridiculous extremes, whose absurdity is obvious. It is rather that there are many factual errors hidden amidst correct information, and much falsehood mixed with truth. How will our pastors be able to distinguish between one and the other? How are they to help their congregations to make such distinctions? If our students do not learn how to do it, how to judge between truth and falsehood, if they cannot help their congregations make such judgments, theological education is not worth much, no matter how much Bible and theology our students may know. In short, the overabundance of both true and false information on the Internet requires a theological education that enables students to practice critical judgment on anything that may appear on the Internet and to do this on solid theological foundations.

Just as the appearance of the printing press in the past led to significant changes in theological curricula, today the presence of the Internet and other digitalized resources forces us to rethink both the curriculum itself and how it is taught. One may take the biblical languages as an example. When the reformers and the generations immediately after them insisted on the need to know those languages in depth, pastors and teachers needed them in order to interpret scripture and to do exegesis. As I have repeatedly stated, I have difficulty understanding how it is possible for us to insist so much on the authority of scripture and not to pay much attention to the languages in which that book is written and on which we supposedly base all our preaching and our theology. However, today there is such an abundance of exegetical resources that perhaps our goal should not be so much to provide students with an in-depth knowledge of Greek and Hebrew, but rather to have them understand the structure of those languages in such a way that they are able to make greater use of the linguistic and exegetical resources available to them in digital form. It is not necessary to know by heart all the conjugations and declensions of the participle of a Greek verb in order to recognize a participle, understand the essence of the morphology before us, and make use of the resources available on the Internet and therefore to reach conclusions that otherwise would be difficult to attain even after long years of studying Greek grammar.

However, what will probably make the most significant impact on future theological education is the manner in which we look at the relation between action and reflection. Modernity, with its emphasis on objectivity, took for granted that in the process of learning, at least in matters such as theology, one must first learn the universally valid content, either factual or theoretical, and then learn how to apply what one now knew. This manner of understanding the relation between learning and practice is clear in what has already be said about the classic German university in which it was expected that the candidate for ordination must first learn theology, Bible, and history at the university, and then go to a different institution in order to learn how all of this is related to the practice of preaching, pastoral care, leading of worship, and so forth. For similar reasons, when I was in seminary, although all students had to serve in nearby churches, this was seen more as an impediment to our studies, as an inevitable interruption more than as part of the learning process. Likewise, when I began to teach at another seminary, now in Puerto Rico, the administration and the faculty bemoaned the fact that our students, instead of being able to devote all their time to study, had to serve in churches that competed with the seminary for their time and attention. Neither in the seminary where I studied nor in the one where I taught was the work that students did in churches closely connected to pedagogical or theological considerations. They were simply unavoidable economic, ecclesiastic, and administrative realities. The most common result was students who learned one thing in the seminary and did something else in the church, students in whom a profound sense of tension between study and practice was implanted—a tension that was sometimes encouraged, although often unwittingly, both by the seminary and by the church.

This resulted in what was then a great advance in theological education, which was called "supervised ministry." According to this model, there was in each faculty at least one person whose responsibility it was to supervise what students did in the churches. Sometimes this was done directly by means of a "director of supervised ministry" and sometimes through indirect supervision, by means of pastors who were to oversee the students' practical work. As today we look back at the history of theological education in the United States—and therefore also in churches resulting from North American missions—we note that one of the main contributions of the second half of the twentieth century was the development of the entire field of supervised ministry.

However there was still something lacking in such supervised ministry. The fundamental vision behind that discipline was that students were to apply in practice what they had learned in theory and relate what they had learned in fields such as biblical and theological studies to the reality of ministry in a local congregation. In other words, it was mostly a linear process, in which the movement went from theory to practice, from academy to church. But today it is commonly held that the best learning process is like a circle, or rather like a spiral, so that theory and practice, action and reflection, have a constant and reciprocal relation. One does not first learn theory and then put it into practice, for practice also affects the manner in which we see, understand, and develop theory, shaping the questions we ask and the methods we follow, while theory constantly has an impact on practice and modifies it.

On the basis of such a vision of the relation between theory and practice, the commitment and participation of students and professors in pastoral tasks, which were earlier seen as an unavoidable necessity making education more diffi-cult, today are seen as an integral part of that very process. This requires the train-ing of a vast number of supervisors who may help students reflect biblically and theologically on their experiences in congregations and bring those experiences to bear on their studies. It also requires an openness on the part of professors of subjects such as Bible, theology, and history, so that they may bring to their class and to their teachings the life of the congregations and the pastoral experi-ences of the students. It also requires a radical reshaping of the criteria by which professors and their scholarship are evaluated. Active participation in the life of the church is not an additional activity side by side with research and reflection, but part of that very research and reflection. It is not just that professors ought to be involved with the church and its ministry out of their own personal com-mitment. It is also that the actual practice of what is taught is just as much a part of research and reflection as is the work done in a library. All of this also requires a radical revision in the curriculum, leaving behind the traditional division into three or four "fields" in which the first ones are academic and the last is practical. If learning is a sort of spiral, in every course or academic activity there must be a practical dimension that is not a mere application of what had been learned but also a determining factor in what and how professors teach and students learn. It is not merely a matter of learning in the classroom how one is to preach but also that in preaching one learns how to approach what is being studied in the classroom—not only in courses on homiletics but also in courses on Bible, theol-ogy, history, and ethics.

In summary, the new times we are facing require a total reorientation and redefinition of theological studies and ministerial training. As we move toward that redefinition, we must take into account both the past experiences and prac-tices of the church and the new circumstances that are emerging. From all of this several general directives arise, which are constitutive elements of a new vision of theological education.

The first such directive is to return theological education to its proper place, which is at the heart of the church—particularly of the church in its local expres-sion, the congregation. Within such a vision, seminaries, faculties of theology in universities, and other programs of theological education certainly do have an important place. But—if they are to be more than schools of religion—this place is to be found in their relationship with the education and reflection that take place within the church, and never above nor apart from it. The best learning takes place in community. But this is not primarily a community of students and teachers, as it was in the very notion of "seminary" that developed in the sixteenth century, but rather the community of faith into which every student and faculty member is grafted.

The second directive is to develop methods of teaching and of evaluating courses that focus less on what one learns than on the manner in which one is able to share and teach both content and the process of learning. Thus for instance, if it were a course on the Creed, a good part of the work the students would do would be to teach in their own communities about the Creed and its significance for life today. Though this would certainly require study and research, the final purpose of the course would not be that students know much about the Creed but rather that they know how to relate what they are learning with their own teaching ministry within their communities of faith.

The third directive is to turn theological education into a life-long process. The goal of theological studies is not a degree or diploma. Their final goal is the contemplation of the face of God in the final reign of peace and justice. Meanwhile, what behooves us is a constant process of reflection both in community and privately, a constant learning about God, God's world, and the purposes and actions of God in the world, as well as a constant growth in obedience and service—that is, a process of sanctification that is spiritual as well as moral and intellectual. Were this directive carried to its conclusion, degrees and diplomas awarded by theological institutions would be valid for a limited period, having to be renewed periodically by giving proof of continuing studying and learning, all within the context of new circumstances as they develop. For many reasons, I have little hope that this will take place in the near future. But, even so, one can underscore the importance of continuing education, as constantly considering new circumstances, new ideas, new methods, and so forth. Within this vision, continuing education is not an ancillary service of a seminary or theological school, but part of its very essence.

The fourth directive is to develop a sort of education that helps the entire church to face constantly evolving circumstances and unexpected challenges. Education must not be content with offering ready-made answers, when we do not even suspect what the questions of tomorrow may be. In order to respond to set questions, instruments such as the *Index of Forbidden Books* of the Roman Catholic Church, or the canonization of ignorance in some Protestant circles, will suffice. But in order to be able to respond to unexpected questions and issues one has to have both basic biblical and theological principles and the flexibility and critical spirit necessary to find new answers to new questions—answers that are faithful to scripture and to theological principles but are also new and even unexpected.

In the fifth place, there is a need to redefine the relationship between theological studies and the practice of ordained ministry—a relationship that in recent centuries has been taken for granted. This must be done in two directions, each of which, while responding to present circumstances, reflects something of the more ancient practices in the history of the church. The first of these two directions is to acknowledge that, as in the case of Saint Augustine, there are a great number of people who seek theological studies, not necessarily in order to practice pastoral ministry but rather to work in various lay ministries or simply better to understand and practice the faith they believe. The second direction leads us to acknowledge that, as in the case of Ambrose, there are a vast number of people who are already in the practice of ministry and who seek theological studies as a means to improve that practice.

The sixth directive is the creation of programs to train mentors in the task of theological reflection and pastoral practice—which does not mean only the practice of the pastor, but even more the pastoral practice of the entire community of faith. For instance, whoever teaches in seminary is to be seen as a mentor to students who in the process become also teachers as well as mentors within their own community of faith. Whoever studies in a seminary must see professors as examples and guides in the process of becoming mentors in their community of faith—a process that must result in new generations of believers/mentors.

Finally, part of the goal of theological education must be to produce and promote materials of study and reflection that may serve as a resource for all the preceding. This will require a redefinition of the criteria by which faculty publications are evaluated, making relevance and usefulness a fundamental criterion. The problem that the church has had to face constantly ever since the invention of the printing press is not a lack of resources but the enormous abundance of resources that are not useful. With the advent of the Internet, this has been greatly multiplied. Throughout the history we have reviewed, we have seen the importance of a number of books—for instance, Augustine's *On Christian Doctrine*, Calvin's *Institutes*, and Barth's *Dogmatics*—as resources that have helped the church respond to the challenges of its time and even beyond. Today we have to do likewise, both by the printed word and by electronic media. Without such resources, the sort of teaching, learning, and reflection proposed above is impossible.

All of this will be extremely difficult, for it will require a radical transformation in the manner in which we think both about academic disciplines and about pastoral practice. It will require significant changes in the manner in which churches relate to seminaries and other programs of pastoral and theological education. As long as there are seminaries that act as if their function were to teach what the church is to believe, and churches that act as if their function were to tell seminaries what they are to teach, it will be difficult to take the first steps toward the reformation both of ministerial education and of the church as a whole—a reformation that in our times has become urgent.

In view of the new realities we see everywhere in our churches as well as in our theological institutions, it is not enough to say that all this will be difficult. Rather, one must confess that it is impossible. There are too many interests at stake. There is too much inertia. There are too many other things that seem more important. But what is impossible for humans is possible for God.

God is already reforming the church. God is reforming it, whether the church wants to be reformed or not. Like it or not, that future is upon us. The Holy Spirit will lead the church along paths of theological education that today we do not even suspect. This does not depend on us but is rather the action and promise of the Lord who said that even the gates of hell—and even less the gates of the twentieth-first century—will not prevail against the church. Therefore, our task for today is not so much to see how we bring about the reformation that God requires and promises but rather how we join it.

16
Bringing It Home

Most observers agree that North American theological education is in crisis. This crisis is multidimensional. Some of its elements are more readily apparent than others. But all are fundamentally important if the church is to develop systems of education that will be viable in the coming decades of the twenty-first century.

The most obvious of the many challenges that theological education faces is financial. There is no doubt that many seminaries are in difficult financial straits and that this threatens some of their core programs and even their very existence. It is difficult to determine how many institutions of theological education are in serious economic difficulties—partly because the definition of "serious difficulties" varies. If by "serious difficulties" one means being in danger of immediate extinction, the number may be relatively small—probably no more than 10 percent of all schools. But there are other manifestations of serious difficulties. Contributions from churches and individuals to the annual budget of theological institutions have been declining for some time. Quite a few of the institutions have been overdrawing on their endowments, and the principal has declined enough that no matter what the stock market does, the financial difficulties of the institution will not be solved. As a result, many have cut programs, reduced staff, frozen salaries, and deferred maintenance. A few have weathered the storm by freezing hiring, or at least limiting it, and by reducing or postponing plans and programs.

In the midst of this crisis, a very select few have managed to expand programs and even to raise their endowment and erect new buildings. They seem to be the exception to the rule, and they have good reason to celebrate. But perhaps such seminaries have an even greater problem: their problem is that they have no problem, and therefore they can temporarily afford the luxury of continuing business as usual, perhaps expanding or modifying a program here or there, but not asking fundamental questions as to how theological education will be shaped in the coming decades. In the long run this crisis may prove more challenging than the crisis of schools now having to find new ways to make ends meet.

Much more serious than the financial crisis is what could be called the ecclesiastical challenge. By this I do not mean simply the complaint that we hear so often, that the seminary is not training its students adequately, that it does not necessarily make them better pastors, and so forth. This complaint has been there for almost as long as seminaries have existed. The way it is usually expressed has overtones of anti-intellectualism, and therefore it is easy to dismiss it, or to become defensive and develop an entire apology trying to show that theological education is indeed relevant and necessary. But this does not mean that we should pay no attention to it, just in case there may be some truth in it.

Those who voice this complaint can easily point out that, as we look at the entire ecclesiastical panorama in the United States, by and large the denominations that traditionally have been most insistent on the need for seminary education in order to practice the pastorate are also the denominations whose membership is most rapidly declining. (The main exception is the Roman Catholic Church, whose membership is increasing, not among its traditional Irish, Polish, and Italian constituency, but mostly due to immigration from Latin America, Vietnam, and the Philippines.) In the late second century the number of those who blamed seminary education for their churches' ills increased to such a point that efforts to "reclaim" the seminaries for the church, and to control what was taught in them, succeeded. This was particularly true among Baptists, where such tendencies had been growing for centuries, even though the oldest free-standing graduate theological seminary—Andover-Newton Theological School—had been founded by Baptists. In many cases, this was accompanied by a tendency to abandon Pietist roots that had long been manifested in much North American theological education and to adopt a more scholastic approach in many ways similar to the Protestant scholasticism of the seventeenth century. A simple explanation—or rather, a simplistic explanation—for all this would be that the reason for this is precisely the aforesaid complaint, that the seminaries are not doing their job properly.

Were that the case, then it would be relatively easy for the theological education establishment and its institutions to respond to the crisis. All that would be necessary would be to make sure that seminary graduates are properly trained for their pastoral tasks and that they are proficient in evangelism and church growth. Indeed, there are a number of institutions that have responded to the challenge at this level.

But the ecclesiastical challenge goes far beyond the complaint that the seminary does not prepare its students adequately. And the needed response also goes far beyond tinkering with the curriculum or adding a few practical courses or strengthening supervised ministry. All of this may be good and even necessary but will not suffice to respond to the challenges we now face.

In truth, the ecclesiastical challenge is rooted in two parallel demographic challenges. The first of these is the population shift from the countryside to the cities and their suburbs. As the rural population decreases, the number of churches that the mainline denominations consider "viable" also decreases. This means that every year there are fewer pulpits to be filled. In the Presbyterian Church in the United States of America, or PC(USA), in the first decade of the twenty-first century the total number of congregations declined by 603, or 5.35 percent. In denominations such as the PC(USA), where churches call their pastors, the result is that a growing number of seminary graduates have difficulty finding a place for ministry. Certainly, the growth of the larger, suburban churches, with their multiple staffs, provides some new possibilities of a call. But this does not suffice to cancel out the number of positions lost as smaller churches find themselves unable to call a pastor. As increasing numbers of graduates are unable to find a call—or at least to find a call that fulfills their vocational goals—the result will be decreasing enrollment. In denominations such as my own United Methodist Church, where pulpits are filled by denominational appointment, the process is different, but the end result is similar. Judicatories in most "mainline" denominations are becoming less aggressive in the recruitment of candidates for ordained ministry, and therefore the number of students whose goal is pastoral ministry is decreasing.

There are a number of ways in which Protestant seminaries seek to respond to this situation. One of the most common and temporarily successful is to develop Doctor of Ministry programs whose students in many cases outnumber those enrolled in the Master of Divinity program. While the Doctor of Ministry is valuable, and seminaries with excellent doctoral programs ought to be commended, simple arithmetic makes it obvious that, as MDiv enrollment wanes, the point of saturation will soon be reached, and the decline in the number of MDiv students will eventually result in a parallel decline in Doctor of Ministry programs. Thus, in the long run seminaries should not count on their DMin programs, no matter how excellent they may be, as a permanent solution to their recruitment shortfalls.

But the second demographic challenge is even more daunting. The class, race, and culture of the traditional members of most "mainline" churches in the United States are no longer as dominant as they were fifty years ago. The number of church members whose denominational connection goes back to their North-European ancestors is waning for two reasons: first, the actual proportion of Euro-Americans within the entire population is decreasing; and, second, a growing number of them are losing touch with their roots, and therefore also with the religious traditions of their progenitors. People who are Presbyterian or Anglican or Methodist or Lutheran because they trace their background to Scotland or to England or to Scandinavia are becoming a smaller proportion both in the nation at large and within the denominations of their immigrant ancestors.

In the ten years before the census of 2010, the Euro-American population of the United States grew by 7.1 percent; the African American, by 11 percent; the Asian American, by 32.3 percent; and the Hispanic American, by 37.1 percent. Obviously, much of the growth of the last two groups is due to immigration. That is certainly the case with the Asian American population, whose median age is about the same as of that of the white population—roughly thirty-six years. But no matter what politicians want to make us believe, the main source of growth for the Latino population is not immigration but rather the birth rate. The median age of the Hispanic population is more than ten years less than the median age of the population at large. The result can be stated starkly: according to the census, for every Euro-American who dies, 1.4 children are born; while for every Latino or Latina who dies, 8.9 children are born! This statistical difference is expected to become even more marked in the next census, for among children under five years of age, more than a quarter are Hispanic and more than a fifth are African American. In other words, by the time some of the younger faculty now teaching in seminaries retire, more than half of the population who will be of an age ready to enter seminary directly after college will be ethnic minorities.

A parallel fact is that, when one looks at membership statistics of major denominations in the United States, one sees not only that their membership is declining but also that if there is any increase, it is among people belonging to ethnic minority backgrounds other than those traditionally associated with a particular denomination. Thus, while Episcopalians, Methodists, and Presbyterians bemoan their declining membership, they would have much more to bemoan were it not for the rapid growth of Korean churches among Presbyterians, of Koreans and Latinos among Methodists, and of immigrants from Africa and the Caribbean who are Anglican. Actually, in the PC(USA) the only synod that reports membership growth is the Synod of Boriquen, in Puerto Rico.

It is also important to note that, even among Euro-Americans, Pentecostal churches and religious traditions that have sprung up in the United States are growing, while those that are more established are waning. Furthermore, there is in much of the Pentecostal community a growing eagerness to study and to learn. This produces the anomaly that the resources in theological education in terms of faculty, libraries, buildings, endowments, and so forth are available mostly to a declining student population, while many searching for better theological education do not have adequate resources.

All of this means that traditional mainline denominations, as well as their seminaries, must begin taking the current demographic challenge more seriously. It will no longer be enough for a denomination to have an office or a department of racial-ethnic minority ministries. It will not be enough to recruit a few ethnic-minority students and faculty. It will be necessary to reexamine the very structure, ethos, and form of government of a denomination, in order to see how these promote or impede its witness in the presently shifting circumstances. Note, for instance, that in order to parallel the ethnic composition of the nation, the African American membership in the Presbyterian Church (USA) would have to quadruple, and the Hispanic membership would have to be multiplied by more than ten. And every year that goes by this situation gets worse.

If one then looks specifically at seminaries, one sees that these demographic trends are having a slight impact. In the last four years, the total enrollment in MDiv programs has remained fairly stable, and most of the increase has taken place among Asian and Hispanic Americans. During a space of five years early in the twenty-first century, the total white enrollment in those programs declined by almost 7 percent, the African American remained the same, the number of Asian Americans increased by 4.5 percent, and Latino enrollment went up by 14 percent. Even so, in 2013 Hispanics were almost 16 percent of the total population, while they were 4.4 percent of MDiv students. If one takes into account that this included some two hundred seminary students in Puerto Rico, the figure for Hispanics in the United States mainland would be 3.8 percent of the total MDiv population.

To take a particular denomination as an example, in 2012, out of 1,443 Presbyterian (USA) MDiv students, approximately 70 (or 5 percent) were Hispanic. (It is also significant to add that the seminaries with the most Presbyterian Hispanic students were not themselves Presbyterian institutions.) And, to be even more specific by taking as an example one of the most prestigious Presbyterian seminaries, at Columbia Theological Seminary in Decatur, Georgia, 2 of 146 MDiv students were Hispanic. This comes to 1.4 percent of the MDiv enrollment, and 1 percent of total enrollment in all programs. African Americans were slightly above 4 percent of MDiv enrollment.

An immediate and most common reaction to such statistics is to enhance recruitment efforts among minorities, frequently by hiring a person—often a part-time person—to recruit minorities. If the success of such a step is limited, at least we have done our part, or perhaps the recruiter was not as efficient as we had hoped. A more enlightened approach tries to be holistic, realizing that in order to recruit minorities one has to combine three elements: efforts at recruitment, increased financial support, and the presence of ethnic minorities among the faculty. But institutions soon find that even this does not suffice, and some go a step further by offering courses and sometimes entire programs in other languages.

Each of these three levels of response is good. But even the last is but a stopgap measure that does not take into account what is happening all around us. The one painful point that the theological education establishment finds most difficult to accept is that the Association of Theological Schools and its member institutions no longer hold the near monopoly on ministerial education that they had just a few decades ago. Back then, except for the Southern Baptists, every major denomination expected that all or most of its clergy would be seminary trained. In more recent times the situation has changed drastically, both in those denominations and in the total picture of Christianity in the United States. Among more traditional Protestant denominations, alternative routes to ordination—or at least to pastoral ministry—have become ever more common, particularly among ethnic minorities.

In my own United Methodist Church, even though the number of Hispanic seminarians is growing, the vast majority of Hispanic pastors follow the alternative path known as the Course of Study. In the Episcopal Church, there is the possibility of "reading for orders." In the Evangelical Lutheran Church in America there is the path to pastoral ministry provided by the project named T.E.E.M.—Theological Education for Emerging Ministries. In the Presbyterian Church (USA), the training of lay pastors, which began as a way to provide leadership for dwindling rural churches, has now become a major way of providing pastoral leadership for ethnic minority churches—particularly immigrant ethnic churches. In short, even among those denominations that require or mostly require a seminary education for their pastoral leadership, the ATS-accredited route no longer has the near monopoly it once had. (To make matters worse, in those denominations that will not allow full ordination for those coming through such alternative routes this is creating dangerous divides in which ethnic minority pastors are often second-class not-quite-members of the clergy.)

This does not take into account the Pentecostal churches that emerged early in the twentieth century and a hundred years later have become a major presence in the total picture of Christianity in the United States. Traditionally, those churches have not required a seminary education of their pastors. Some have even discouraged it. In more recent times, however, many of these attitudes have changed, leading to a new interest in formal studies. Part of the reason is that, like the church in its early centuries, they are often challenged by movements and claims that, while similar to traditional Pentecostalism in many ways, seem to depart from the faith of the Pentecostal movement as a whole. Over the years, Pentecostal churches have developed a vast number of Bible institutes and Bible colleges that now produce the majority of their pastors. The result is that, in the entire picture of theological education in the United States, ATS-style theological education is no longer normative.[1] In any of our major cities there are several hundred churches whose pastors never went to seminary, but rather to a Bible institute or a Bible college—and even many who have no formal theological education at all.

Thus, while the picture of ministerial education in the Unites States is becoming increasingly complex, the traditional place and role of mainline seminaries is rapidly changing. Change can be costly and painful. But those institutions that do not recognize the urgent need for change will be left behind.

This may be illustrated by an example drawn from the parallel history of two schools in New York City, New York Theological Seminary (NYTS) and Union Theological Seminary. In the mid-twentieth century, NYTS was in deep trouble and on the verge of closing. In contrast, Union was flourishing. It boasted the largest theological library in the Western Hemisphere. The Union library system of cataloguing was the standard for theological libraries all over the nation and even overseas. When Union professors such as Reinhold Niebuhr and Paul Tillich spoke, the *New York Times* and the entire nation took notice. In brief, while New York Theological was floundering, Union was flourishing.

The crisis at NYTS was so profound that the school called a new president with the freedom and the mandate to change whatever was necessary. That new president was familiar with the changing demographics of the city and set to work developing an institution that would respond to the new conditions. Since many among the ethnic minority population did not have the necessary academic credentials, agreements were made with an accredited college to facilitate the process, qualifying students to enter more advanced programs at the seminary. Classes were begun in Spanish and Korean, and later in French and Haitian Creole. The class schedule was adjusted so that African Americans, Hispanics, and other generally impoverished minorities could attend in the evenings and on Saturdays. To open the doors of theological education to a growing incarcerated population, by the mid-1980s an extension program was begun inside the Sing Sing Correctional Facility.

Meanwhile, at Union things began to decline. No longer did the voice of its professors command the widespread attention it once did. Eventually, the only way for Union to maintain its very prestigious programs was to overdraw on the endowment. Then it became necessary to sell part of the beautiful campus, to rent other parts, and to turn its famed library into part of the Columbia University Library System.

By 2012, the total enrollment in all degree programs at Union was 253, while NYTS had 390 enrolled in its ATS-accredited seminary degrees and another

270 in other programs. At that point Union was engaged in efforts to do what should have been done decades earlier. But this promised to be an uphill struggle.

There is no doubt that there is a crisis looming for theological education as most of us have known it. Such theological education reflects a history of some fifteen centuries during which the church could count on the generally supportive attitude of its cultural and social environment. It is the heir of monastic and cathedral schools, of medieval universities, of post-Reformation seminaries and universities. This is a grand legacy, and one that must not be lost, for it is part of our identity. Yet it is also a legacy that may make it difficult for us to respond to the present shifting situation, when we can no longer take for granted that the surrounding culture and society are supportive, as they were when most of our theological schools were founded.[2]

This new context has several dimensions. For a number of economic and cultural reasons, the demographic shift also means that the proportion of people with a college degree in any of the liberal arts is diminishing. Thus, it will be increasingly difficult to sustain a theological education that is generally reserved for such people.

Then, there is the religious illiteracy of the population at large. Without much exaggeration, one may say that there are in our society growing numbers of people who know about the Christian faith just about as much as did a moderately informed pagan in the third century.

Taken together, these two factors mean that traditionally accredited theological education runs the risk of becoming just as elitist and as generally irrelevant as were the medieval universities by the fifteenth century or the scholastic Protestant universities by the eighteenth.

If we are to respond to such challenges, there is much we can learn from the practice of the church at a time when it found itself in a nonsupportive context.

First of all, we must learn that theological education must be a continuum, leading from catechetical teaching, through the continued education and growth in discipleship of the entire church, to the training of pastors and other leaders, to the most sophisticated levels of research and reflection.

Second, we must challenge the modern model in which theory precedes practice and make room for an action-reflection-action circular model similar to what Ambrose and Augustine had to follow when they were unexpectedly ordained. Ambrose knew little or no theology and had to learn it as he practiced ministry. Augustine was already an accomplished theologian, but the actual practice of ministry forced him to correct much of his theology.

Third, mostly as a consequence of the first two, we need to set aside the elitism that so often plagues us and our institutions. As part of a continuum, we must learn to judge our work not on the basis of how difficult or how exclusive our admissions are (or on the GPA of those we admit) but rather on the manner in which we communicate with that entire continuum.

Fourth, we must realize that the relationship between study and ordination is not as clear-cut as we have made it. Throughout most of the history of the church, even the highest levels of theological education have not necessarily led to ordination, and ordination has often preceded advanced studies. The best theological study is motivated primarily not by the need to satisfy requirements for ordination but by the love of God. We study theology because we seek better to know and to serve the God whom we love—and this is a motivation equally present among the laity and among those ordained or seeking ordination.

Fifth, it should be clear to all that the number of commuting and part-time students is increasing and will continue to increase and that therefore a major factor in deciding where to pursue theological studies is location and ease of access. While the residential, full-time model that recruits students from a wide area has an undeniable value and should continue, seminaries and schools of theology will need to establish closer ties with their immediate communities, knowing their needs, and offering programs, schedules, and other options that meet those needs.

Sixth, as a consequence of all the foregoing, ATS-accredited theological institutions must find ways to encourage and acknowledge the work done in responsible but not accredited programs, for it is out of such programs that the vast majority of Protestant pastors are emerging and will emerge in the future. (At the time of this writing, there were in North Georgia twenty-one Hispanic United Methodist churches, and only two of their pastors were seminary graduates.)

Seventh, while denominational schools must continue preserving and transmitting the values of their own traditions and confessions, they must widen their ecclesiastical and denominational horizons. This must be done intentionally, systematically, institutionally, and urgently.

And finally, as part of that widening of horizons, we must acknowledge the cultural captivity of much of our institutional and ecclesiastical life, which prevents us from recruiting and making way for the growing minorities that will soon be the majority of the church. Difficult as this may be, it is necessary if our institutions are to remain viable and relevant in the decades to come.

Notes

1. The Early Church

1. William V. Harris, *Ancient Literacy* (Cambridge, MA: Harvard University Press, 1989), 272.

2. Harris, *Ancient Literacy*, 320–21.

3. Cyprian, *Epistle* 29.2. (*Epistle* 28 or 35 in other editions). This is my own translation.

2. The Catechumenate

1. Justin Martyr, *The First Apology*, 61, in vol. 1 of *The Ante-Nicene Fathers*, ed. Alexander Roberts and James Donaldson (Grand Rapids: Eerdmans, 2001), 183. Hereafter this series will be abbreviated as *ANF*.

2. Tertullian, *The Prescription against Heretics*, 41, in *ANF*, 3:263. In order to understand these words, it helps to know that catechumens were not admitted to Communion, nor to the "prayers of the people," in which the church, as the priestly people of God, interceded for the world. Tertullian is complaining that heretics do not follow this practice.

3. Early Christian baptismal practices must be pieced together from several sources. One of these is *The Apostolic Tradition* of Hippolytus. Although known in the nineteenth century as an ancient text, supposedly of Egyptian origin, scholars in the twentieth century determined that this was indeed the work of Hippolytus and therefore older than was supposed. In the second half of the twentieth century, this led to a more detailed understanding of early Christian

141

catechetical and baptismal practices. It is one of the main sources employed in this chapter.

4. Cyril, *Procatechesis*, prologue, 1 (AT).

5. Ibid., prologue, 17 (AT).

6. Saint Augustine's sermons 61–69 are to be read within this context, which they illumine.

7. Augustine, Sermon 227, trans. Edmund Hill, in *The Works of Augustine: A Translation for the 21st Century*, ed. John E Rotelle (Hyde Park, NY: New City Press), 6:254.

8. Sermon 228, in ibid., 6:262.

3. From Constantine to the Germanic Invasions

1. Tertullian, *On Baptism*, 18, in *ANF* 3:678.

2. Ambrose, *On the Duties of the Clergy*, 2.6.25, in vol. 10 of *The Nicene and Post-Nicene Fathers*, Series 2, ed. Philip Schaff and Henry Wace (Grand Rapids: Eerdmans, 1978), 47. Hereafter this series will be abbreviated as *NPNF2*.

3. Ibid., 1.1.4, in *NPNF2*, 10:1.

4. Ibid., 1.1.3, in *NPNF2*, 10:1.

5. Jerome, *Commentary on Ezekiel*, preface to book 3, in *NPNF2*, 6:500.

6. Jerome, *Letter 127*, "To Principia," 12, in *NPNF2*, 6:256.

7. Augustine, *On Christian Doctrine*, preface, 1 (AT).

8. Ibid., preface, 4, 8 (AT).

9. Augustine, *De magistro*, 11.36 (AT).

10. Ibid., 11.38 (AT).

4. The Romanization of the Germanic Peoples

1. Braulio of Zaragoza, quoted in Manuel C. Díaz y Díaz, "Introducción general," *Etimologías de Isidoro de Sevilla* (Madrid: B.A.C., 1982), 214.

2. Gregory the Great, *Pastoral Rule*, 1.1 (AT).

3. Ibid., 1.2 (AT).

4. Ibid., 2.4 (AT).

5. Ibid., 2.6 (AT).

5. Early Medieval Schools

1. See, for instance, Benedict of Nursia, *Rule*, 8.8 and 48.22.

2. Bede, *Ecclesiastical History of England*, 3.27, trans. John Stevens, ed. by J. A. Giles (London: Bohn, 1847), 162–63.

3. Finian, *Penitential*, 3, in John T. McNeill and Helena M. Gamer, trans., *Medieval Handbooks of Penance* (New York: Columbia University Press, 1990), 88.

4. Finian, *Penitential*, 10, in McNeill and Gamer, *Medieval Handbooks of Penance*, 89.

5. Finian, *Penitential, 23*, in McNeill and Gamer, *Medieval Handbooks of Penance*, 91. At this time, one should point out that the penance of exile as penalty for homicide was one of the reasons that led some Irish monks—among them the famous Columba, founder of the Iona community—to be missionaries both in Great Britain and on the continent.

6. See Justo L. González, *A History of Christian Thought*, vol. 2 (Nashville: Abingdon Press, 1987), 107–42.

6. The Beginnings of Scholasticism

1. Anselm, *Proslogion*, 1, in *A Scholastic Miscellany: Anselm to Ockham*, ed. Eugene R. Fairweather (Philadelphia: The Westminster Press, 1956), 73.

2. Hugh of Saint Victor, *Didascalicon*, 3.7 (AT).

3. Peter Lombard, *Sentences* I, *proemium* (AT).

4. Ibid (AT).

5. Ibid (AT).

7. The Universities and Scholasticism

1. Quoted in Ray C. Perry, ed., *A History of Christianity: Readings in the History of the Early and Medieval Church* (Englewood Cliffs, NJ: Prentice-Hall, 1962), 409.

2. Bonaventure, *On the Excellence of Christ's Teaching*, 3 (AT).

3. Thomas Aquinas, *Summa Theologica*, trans. Fathers of the English Dominican Province (New York: Benziger Bros., 1948), part 1, question 111, articles 1, 3; question 117, article 1; and part 2-2, question 181, article 3.

4. Ibid., part 1, question 117, article 1.

5. Bonaventure, *Breviloqium, proemium*, 6.5 (AT).

8. The Last Centuries of the Middle Ages

1. Although it is frequently said that Luther was the first who wrote, or at least the first to publish, a catechism, this not true. Among others, Jean Gerson (1363–1429) composed an *ABC for Simple People*. And in 1470 the monk Theodoric Dederich had the first German catechism published under the title of *Christenspiegel—Christian Mirror*.

2. There is an excellent study about how this functioned in Burgos, which serves to illustrate what took place in the rest of Europe: Susana Guijarro González, "Jerarquía y redes sociales en la Castilla medieval," in *Anuario de Estudios Medievales*, 38, no. 1 (enero–junio, 2008): 271–99.

3. The data in this section are taken from José Luis Martín Martín, "Alfabetización y poder del clero secular de la Península Ibérica en la Edad Media," in Peter Burke, José Luis Martín Martín, et al., *Educación y transmisión de conocimientos en la historia* (Salamanca: Ediciones Universidad, 2002), 95–143.

4. Besides being dark skinned, El Tostado was also extremely short. It is said that in a council, when he stood up to speak, someone shouted: *surge*—stand up—to which the prelate answered: *ego non sum plus*—I am no more than this.

5. It seems that this term was coined by Johan Huizinga in 1919 in his classic work *Herfsttij del Middeleuwen*, translated into English as *The Waning of the Middle Ages* (London: E. Arnold, 1924).

6. A phrase that served as the title of the famous book by Heiko Oberman, *Herbst der mittelalterliche Theologie*, published in English as *The Harvest of Medieval Theology* (Cambridge, MA: Harvard University Press, 1963).

7. Philippe Delhaye, *Christian Philosophy in the Middle Ages* (London: Burns & Oates, 1960), 113.

9. In Quest of Alternatives

1. John van Engen, trans., in *Devotio Moderna* (New York: Paulist Press, 1998), 65.

2. Thomas à Kempis, *The Imitation of Christ*, 1.1.2 (Garden City, NY: Image Books, 1955), 31–32.

3. Ibid., 3.43.1, pp. 165–66.

4. Ibid., 3.43.3, p. 166.

10. The Protestant Reformation

1. Prologue to the German translation of Melanchthon's *Commentary on Colossians*, 1529, in Harold H. Lentz, *Reformation Crossroads: A Comparison of the Theology of Luther and Melanchthon* (Minneapolis: Augsburg, 1958), 3.

2. Letter from Martin Luther, quoted in Clyde L. Manschreck, *Melanchthon: The Quiet Reformer* (New York: Abingdon Press, 1958), 24.

3. R. Keen, *A Melanchthon Reader* (New York: Peter Lang, 1988), 50.

4. Philipp Melanchton, *School Order for the Schools of Mecklenburg*, quoted in C. L. Robins, *Teachers in Germany in the Sixteenth Century* (New York: Columbia University, 1912), 106.

5. Conrad Bergendoff, ed., *Luther's Works*, vol. 40 (Philadelphia: Muhlenberg Press. 1958), 293–94.

6. Ibid., 40:314.

7. John Calvin, *Commentary on Psalms*, in *Ioannis Calvini Opera Quae Supersunt Omnia*, vol. 3, ed. Guilielmus Baum, Eduardus Cunitz, and Eduardus

Reuss, Corpus Reformatorum 31 (Brunsvigae: C. A. Schwetschke et Filium, 1865), 31.24.

8. John Calvin, *Ordonances de 1541*, in John Calvin, *Homme d'église: Oeuvres choisies du réformateur et documents sur les églises réformées du XVIᵉ siècle* (Genève: Éditions Labor, 1936), 34.

11. The Catholic Reformation

1. *Constitutions*, 4.3.1 (AT).

2. *Ratio studiorum et Institutiones Scholasticae Societatis Iesu* (Romae: Collegio Societis Iesu, 1599), 1, 5 (AT).

3. See Miguel Beltrán-Quera, *La pedagogía de los jesuitas en la Ratio studiorum* (Caracas: Universidad Católica Andrés Bello, 1984).

4. Ibid., 395.

12. Protestant Scholasticism and Rationalism

1. See Howard Hotson, *Johann Heinrich Alsted, 1588–1638: Between Renaissance, Reformation, and Universal Reform* (New York: Oxford University Press, 2002).

2. François Turretin, *Institutio theologiae elenticae*, 1.6.5 (Ludg. Batavor: Fredericum Harring, 1696), 1:21.

3. Johann Gerhard, *On the Ecclesiastical Ministry*, vol. 2, Theological Commonplaces 26.10, trans. Richard J. Dinda (Saint Louis: Concordia Publishing House, 2012), 281.

4. See John Morgan, *Godly Learning: Puritan Attitudes towards Reason, Learning and Education, 1560–1640* (Cambridge: Cambridge University Press, 1986), particularly 103–17.

5. F. W. B. Bullock, *A History of Training for the Ministry of the Church of England and Wales from 1800 to 1874* (St. Leonards-on-the-Sea: Budd & Gillat, 1955), 4.

13. The Pietist Reaction

1. John Wesley, *The Works of John Wesley*, ed. Thomas Jackson (London: Wesleyan Methodist Book Room, 1872), 4:450.

14. Modern Theological Education

1. Friedrich Schleiermacher, in a letter dated August 19, 1802, quoted in Martin Redeker, *Schleiermacher: Life and Thought* (Philadelphia: Fortress, 1973), 9.

2. Austin Flannery, ed., *Vatican Council II*, vol. 1, *The Conciliar and Postconciliar Documents* (Dublin, Ireland: Dominican Publications, 1996), 719–20.

15. A Brief Overview

1. Anselm, *Proslogion*, 1, in *A Scholastic Miscellany: Anselm to Ockham*, ed. Eugene R. Fairweather (Philadelphia: The Westminster Press, 1956), 73.

16. Bringing It Home

1. As this book goes to press, the Asociación para la Educación Teológica Hispana (AETH) and ATS are beginning the process to implement an agreement whereby graduates of certain Bible institutes certified by AETH will be able to enter ATS institutions as with a college degree. This has the potential of producing a dramatic increase in the number of Hispanics applying at ATS seminaries in future years.

2. In 2011, a Global Survey on Theological Education was launched. The report of this survey to the World Council of Churches, whose assembly took place in late 2013, shows on the one hand the degree to which theological education in the younger churches seeks to imitate models brought by missionaries from the North Atlantic and on the other the vast number of experiments that are taking place precisely in regions where the church has seldom or never had the support it traditionally had within Christendom. It may well be that some of the experiments in the younger churches will serve to reform and renew theological education in the United States and in Europe.

Index

abbots and abbesses, 31
Abelard, Peter, 37, 38, 39, 40, 43, 46
Academy of Athens, 4
action and reflection, 125–27, 138
Adagia (Erasmus), 68
Adelm of Sherborne, 31
Adeodatus, 21
Adler, Alfred, 110
Adrianapolis, battle of, 17
Agapitus, 24
Agder, Council of (506), 15
Alcalá de Henares, University of, 67,
    82–83
Alcuin of York, 31, 33–34
Alexander II, 30
Alexander IV, 49
Alexander of Hales, 48
Alexandria, catechetical school of, 5–6,
    22
Alsted, Johann Heinrich, 89–90
alternative routes to ordination, 136
Ambrose, 3, 16–17, 18, 22, 119, 138
Anabaptism, 77
Andover-Newton Theological School,
    132
Anselm, 30, 37–38, 52, 118
antinomian, 73
Apostolic Tradition, The (Hippolytus),
    141
Arabic, 100
Aramaic, 100
Aristotelian logic, 88, 89

Aristotle, 50, 51
Arius, 6
Arminians, 88
Asociación para la Educación Teológica
    Hispana, 147
Association of Theological Schools, 136,
    137–39, 147
audientes, 10–11
Augustine of Canterbury, 30
Augustine of Hippo, 3, 4, 13, 15, 17,
    19–22, 34, 35, 50, 52, 58, 75,
    122, 138
Augustinian tradition, 39, 51
Averroes, 50
Avila, 57, 58

Bacon, Robert, 48
baptism, 10–13, 16–17, 56, 141–42
    of infants, 17
bards, 31
Baronius, Cesar, 89
Basel, University of, 77
Basil the Great (of Caesarea), 3, 4
Bec, Abbey of, 30, 37
Bede, the Venerable, 31
Bellarmine, Robert, 89
Benedict of Nursia, 30
benefice, 56–57, 58–59, 63
Berlin, University of, 106, 107, 109,
    110, 120
Bern, 76
Bernard of Clairvaux, 38

Beza, Theodore, 76–77
Bible colleges, 136–37
Bible institutes, 136–37
biblical imperialism, 112, 121
biblical languages, 100. *See also* Hebrew,
    study of; Greek, study of; Latin
bishops, 4, 31, 81, 114
Bologna, University of, 44
Bonaventure, 47, 49, 50–51, 52
Borromeo, Charles, 81–82
Brethren of the Common Life, 63–68,
    82
Breviloquium (Bonaventure), 52
Brief Outline of Theological Studies
    (Schleiermacher), 106
British Isles, 75
Bucer, Martin, 75, 98
Bullinger, Heinrich, 75, 76

Calov, Abraham, 89
Calvin, John, 59, 75–77, 87, 119
Calvinism, 89
canonization of ignorance, 110, 112,
    121, 128
Canons of Saint Augustine, 19–20, 38,
    122
Carolingians, 29, 33–35
cases of conscience, 90
Cassiodorus, Magnus Aurelius, 24–25,
    33, 35, 119
catechism, 56
Catechism (Calvin), 75
Catechisms of Luther, 72–73
catechumenate, 9–14, 118
    decline of, 15–16, 22
    duration of, 11
cathedral schools, 29–33, 35, 43–44,
    58, 119, 122
    of Paris, 38, 39, 43–44
challenges to contemporary theological
    education
    demographic, 133–37
    ecclesiastical, 132–33

financial, 131–33
Charlemagne, 33–35
Charles the Bald, 35
Christian education, 111, 118
Christian Library (Wesley), 101, 119
Cicero, 4, 18
City of God (Augustine), 20
Clement of Alexandria, 6
collegia pietatis, 98
Collegium Germanicum, 80
collegium philobiblicum, 99
Columba, 143
Columbia University, 137
Comenius, John Amos, 92–93
Communion, 13, 16
community living, 49, 63, 82, 84,
    119–20, 122, 127–28
comparative religions, 106
competentes, 11–12
Complutensian Polyglot Bible, 67, 79
confession, private, 31
Confession of Westminster, 88
confirmation, 56
Confraternity of Christian Doctrine (da
    Castello), 79
Constantine, 15–16
Constantinople, fall of, 66
Constitutions (Jesuit), 80
contemplation and learning, 22, 52
continuing education, 128
Cornelius, 9–10
correctoria, 60
Course of Study, 102, 136
Creed, 12
Crescentius, 5
cryptocalvinists, 88
curriculum, university and seminary
    contemporary, 110–11, 113, 125,
        127, 133
    in the Middle Ages, 46–47
    Melanchthon's, 71–72, 74
    Lutheran, 89–90
    Pietist, 98–100

Puritan, 91
Schleiermacher's, 106–7
Cyprian, 4, 122
Cyril of Jerusalem, 12, 15

D'Abbeville, Gerard, 49
da Castello, Castellino, 79
d'Ailly, Pierre, 61
deacons, 4
Dederich, Theodoric, 144
De formandis concionibus sacris, 74
Deism, 92
De magistro (Augustine), 21–22, 50
De magistro (Aquinas), 50–51
Demetrius, 6
De ratio verae theologiae (Erasmus), 67
Descartes, René, 91, 93
devotio moderna, 64–66, 67
Dewey, John, 111
Didactica magna (Comenius), 92
digitalized resources, 125
Discourse on Method (Descartes), 91
disputatio de quodlibet, 45, 46–47, 50
disputatio ordinaria, 45, 47
disputationes, 44, 83. *See also disputatio
    de quodlibet; disputatio ordinaria*
Doctor of Ministry, 133
dogmatics, 106
Dominic, Saint, 48, 52
Dominicans, 47–48, 49, 60, 70, 122
Dort, Synod of, 88, 89
Duns Scotus, John, 59, 60

Easter, 11, 13
Ecclesiatical Ordinances (Calvin), 76
ecclesiolae in ecclesia, 98
Elizabeth I, 81
eloquentia perfecta, 84
Elvira, Council of (305), 11, 15
empiricism, 92
Enchiridion (Augustine), 20
endowments, 131, 134, 137
England, 30, 76

Enlightenment, 105, 107
Episcopal Church, 134, 136
Erasmus, Desiderius, 64, 66–68
Erfurt, University of, 77, 98–99
ethics, 90
Eustoquium, 18
Evangelical Lutheran Church, 136
evangelical poverty, debates on, 49–50

faith and reason, 60
fasting, 32
feeling of dependence on God, 106–7
Fernández de Madrigal, Alonso, 58
feudalism, 56
Finian, penitential of, 32
flagellants, 65
formation, 84, 113, 123
Formula of Concord, 88
Fourth Lateran Council, 40
Francis, Saint, 48, 52
Franciscans, 47, 60, 122
Francke, August Hermann, 98–100
Frankfort, council of (794), 34
Frederick I of Prussia, 98, 99
Freud, Sigmund, 110
Fribourg, University of, 77
Fromm, Erich, 110
fundamentalism, 109, 111

Gefühl, 106
Geneva, Academy of, 75–77
Gerhard, Johann, 89, 90
Germanic invasions, 16, 23
Germany, 33, 75
Gerson, Jean, 144
Glaubenslehre (Schleiermacher), 106
Global Survey on Theological
    Education, 147
God fearers, 9–10
Great Britain, 109, 119
Greater Catechism (Luther), 72–73
Grebel, Conrad, 77
Greek, study of, 66–67, 70, 71, 75, 77,
    91

Greek, study of (*continued*)
  New Testament, 67
Gregory of Nazianzus, 4
Gregory the Great, 15, 24–25, 26–27,
  30, 119
Gregory the Wonderworker, 6
Greifswald, University of, 72
Groote, Gerard, 63–64

Hadrian VI, 64
Halle, University of, 98–100, 101, 120
Harvard University, 91, 109, 110
Hebrew, study of, 67, 70, 75, 77, 91
Hegel, G. W. F., 108
Hegelianism, 108
Hermas, 2
Hilda, abbess of Whitby, 33
Hippolytus, 141
historical critical method, 108, 109
historical theology, 106–7
Hodge, Charles, 110
Hoffman, Melchoir, 77
Hohenzollern, house of, 98
homiletics, 74, 89, 109, 111
Hubmaier, Balthasar, 77
Hugh of Saint Victor, 37, 38–39, 46
humanism, 66–68, 70, 79, 80, 82, 83,
  84
Hume, David, 106
Hungary, 75
Huns, 29
Hyperius, Andreas, 74, 89

Iberian Peninsula, 57
Ignatius Loyola, 80, 82–83
Ignatius of Antioch, 3
illumination, 50, 51
Imitation of Christ (Thomas à Kempis),
  65, 66
Index of Forbidden Books, 124, 128
infralapsarianism, 95
Ingolstadt, University of, 77
Innocent III, 40, 44

Institutes of the Christian Religion
  (Calvin), 75, 119, 124
*Instructions for the Visitors of Parish Pas-
  tors in Electoral Saxony*, 73
Internet, 123, 124–25, 129
inwardness, 66
Ireland, 29, 31–32
Isidore of Seville, 24, 25–26
Islam, 29. *See also* Muslim

Janus linguarum reserata, 92
Jean de Saint Giles, 48
Jena, University of, 72
Jerome, 5, 17, 18–19, 34, 58, 67
Jesuits, 64, 80, 82–85
Jiménez de Cisneros, Francisco, 67, 79,
  82–83
John of Saxony, 73
Jung, Carl, 110
Justin Martyr, 5, 10, 11

Kant, Immanuel, 105, 106
knowledge, theory of, 50–51
Köln, University of, 77
Königsberg, University of, 72
Korean Presbyterian and Methodist
  churches in the United States, 134

Lanfranc, 30
Latin, 23, 66–67, 70, 71, 75, 77, 91
Latin America, 80
Latino Methodist churches in the
  United States, 134
Lausanne, 76
lay preachers, 101
lectio, 44
Leipzig, University of, 99
Lent, 11
León, council in, 57
Lesser Catechism (Luther), 73
*Letter to the Councilmen of All the Ger-
  man Cities* (Luther), 71
liberal arts, 24–25, 35, 39, 46, 70, 76,
  83, 91

liberalism, 109, 111
libertinism, 73
literacy, 2–3
Locke, John, 92
Logica Theologica (Alsted), 89
Lombard, Peter, 37, 39–40, 44, 58
Louis IX, 49
Louvain, University of, 67
Lucian of Antioch, 6
Luther, Martin, 19, 64, 69–70, 71,
    72–73, 87, 88, 124
Lutheranism, 88

Machen, John Gresham, 110
Magyars, 29
maieutic, 21
mainline denominations, 133
Mammea, Julia, 6
Marburg, University of, 72
Marsilio of Padua, 61
Martel, Charles, 29
Mary Tudor, 81
Mastricht, Peter van, 90–91
Maurus, Hrabanus, 34–35, 71
Melanchthon, Phillip, 69–74, 87, 88
Melito of Sardis, 3
mendicant orders, 47
Menno Simons, 77
mentors, 119, 129
Methodism, 101–2, 120
Milan, 81
modernism, 108
modernity, 89, 91, 108, 109, 111, 125
monastic schools, 29–32, 34, 35,
    43–44, 47, 119, 122
monasticism, 18–20, 22, 24–25, 63,
    82, 84
monetary economy, 37
Moravians, 92, 95, 100, 105
Muslim, 37, 52

Neoplatonism, 4
Netherlands, 75, 76

New World, 79
New York Theological Seminary,
    137–38
Nicholas of Cusa, 64
Normans, 29, 31, 33, 35, 37
novitiate, 30
Noyon, 59

objectivity, 108, 109, 120, 125
oblates, 30
On Christian Doctrine (Augustine),
    20–21, 35
Oporto, council in, 57
Optatam totius, 114
Optatus, 5
orders, major and minor, 55–56
Origen, 6
original sin, 17
Orthodox Presbyterian Church, 110
Oxford, University of, 44, 48, 101, 122

Pantenus, 6
Papias of Hierapolis, 3
Paris
    Dominican house in, 48–50
    University of, 40, 44, 47, 50, 77, 83,
        122
Parisian method, 82–83
parochial schools, 33, 34, 47, 55
pastoral care, 90
pastoral psychology, 110–11
Pastoral Rule (Gregory), 26–27
Paula, 18
penitential books, 31–32
Pentecostal churches in the United
    States, 134, 136–37
Philippists, 88
philosophy and theology, 39, 51, 64,
    71, 82–83, 106
philosophy of religion, 106
Pia desideria (Spener), 96–98
Pietism, 95–103, 105, 120
Pius, 2

Pius IV, 81
Platonism, 51
Polainos of Zura, 3
Pole, Reginald, 80–81
Polycarp of Smyrna, 3
population in the United States, by race, 134
potentia Dei absoluta, 60
potentia Dei ordinata, 60
practical theology, 107, 108–9, 110–11
praelectio, 83
prayers of the people, 13
Presbyterian Church, 110, 133, 135, 136
Presbyteriorum ordinis, 114
presbyters, 4
priesthood of believers, 97
primogeniture, 33
Princeton University, 110
printing press, 64, 66, 73, 84, 124
Protestant Reformation, 69–77, 120
psychology, 110
publish or perish, 113
Puritanism, 91

quadrivium, 25, 34, 46
quaestiones disputatae. See disputationes
Quinian, penitential of, 32

radical reformation, 77
rationalism, 91–92
Ratio studiorum (Jesuits), 82–85
reading for orders, 136
recruitment of minorities, 135–36
Reformed tradition, 75, 76
renunciations, 12
repetition, 83
Reuchlin, Johannes, 70
rhetoric, 2, 3, 25, 26, 58, 83, 91, 117
Richard of Saint Victor, 38
Roland of Cremona, 48
Roman Catholic Church membership, 132

Romanticism, 105
Rome, Seminary of, 81
Rule (Benedict), 30

Saint Victor, school of, 38–39, 43
Salamanca, University of, 44, 122
Salerno, University of, 44
sanctification, 128
Saturus, 5
Saxony, 98
Schleiermacher, Friedrich, 105–8, 110–11
scholarships, 59
scholasticism, 37–41, 43–53, 59–61, 84
   Protestant, 87–91, 92, 93, 132
School Order for the Schools of Mecklenburg (Melanchthon), 72
Schwenkfeld, Caspar, 77
Scotland, 76
scripture, interpretation of, 2, 20, 25, 74
scrutinies, 12
Second Vatican Council, 114–15
Segovia, 58
seminaries, 80–82, 114, 117, 119, 122–23
   minor and major, 82
   with courses in various languages, 136
Sentences (Lombard), 39–40, 44, 46, 58
   Commentaries on, 51
Service of the Word, 13
Sic et non (Abelard), 38, 39, 46
Simplician, 3, 18
sinecure, 58
Sing Sing Correctional Facility, 137
Sisters of the Common Life, 63, 64
slaves, 2
Slavs, 29
Society of Jesus. *See* Jesuits
Socrates, 21
Southern Baptists, 136
specialization, 111–14, 120

Spener, Philipp Jakob, 96–98
Spinoza, Baruch, 105
Spiritual Exercises (Ignatius Loyola), 85
Strasbourg, 75
  University of, 96, 109
Strum, Jean, 75
Summa Contra Gentiles (Thomas
  Aquinas), 52
Summa Theologica (Thomas Aquinas),
  50–51
supervised ministry, 126
supralapsarianism, 95
Switzerland, 75
synoptic problem, 108

Tatian, 5
teacher, function of, 21, 50–51, 76, 84,
  129
Tempier, Étienne, 58
Tertullian, 10, 16
textual criticism, 67
Theodoric, 24
Theodulf of Orleans, 33
theology, purpose of, 52
theory and practice, 126–27
Thirty-Years War, 88
Thomas à Kempis, 64, 65
Thomas Aquinas (Saint Thomas), 39,
  47, 48, 50–51, 52, 60, 83, 114
Toledo, Second Council of, 33
Trent, Council of, 79–81, 113–14, 119,
  122–23
trivium, 25, 34, 46, 58
Turretin, François, 90

Ulfilas, 16
Ulloa y de Fonseca, Alonso, 57

Union Theological Seminary, 110,
  137–38
United Methodist Church, 102, 136
United States, 102, 109, 119, 126
universities, 41, 43–54, 88, 117, 119,
  120, 122

Vaison, Third Council of, 33
Valencia, 58
Valerius of Hippo, 4, 19
Valladolid, council in, 57
vernacular languages, 64
Vetus Latina, 19
Vienna, University of, 77
Vincent de Paul, 114
Visigoths, 17, 18–20, 33
Vulgate, 19, 22

Wesley, John, 101–2, 119, 120
Westminster Theological Seminary, 110
Whitefield, George, 102
William of Auvergne, 58
William of Champeaux, 38, 43
William of Ockham, 60, 61
William of Saint Amour, 49
Windesheim, 64
Wittenberg, University of, 69–74, 100
women, 2, 63, 64, 99, 101
World Council of Churches, 147

Yale University, 109, 110

Zinzendorf, Nicholas von, 95, 100–101
Zürich, 77
Zwingli, Ulrich, 77

CPSIA information can be obtained at www.ICGtesting.com
Printed in the USA
LVOW06s0012101115

461726LV00005B/74/P